As the Twig Is Bent

Harold Steindam

As
THE TWIG
IS BENT

SERMONS FOR CHILDREN

Illustrated by J. Parker Heck

THE PILGRIM PRESS · NEW YORK

Scripture quotations are from the *Revised Standard Version of the
Bible,* copyright 1946, 1952 and © 1971 by the Division of Christian
Education, National Council of Churches, and are used by permission.
The trade name Pringle's is used in sermon 23 by permission of The
Procter & Gamble Company.

Library of Congress Cataloging in Publication Data

Steindam, Harold, 1950-
  As the twig is bent.

  Includes index.
  Summary: Fifty-two sermons on Christian living to be
delivered to children throughout the liturgical year.
  1. Children's sermons. [1. Sermons. 2. Christian life]
I. Heck, J. Parker, ill.   II. Title.
III. Title: Sermons for children.
BV4315.S684   1983   252'.53   83-13734
ISBN 0-8298-0679-2 (pbk.)

The Pilgrim Press, 132 West 31 Street, New York, New York 10001

TO
the beautiful children
of
Emanuel United Church of Christ
Upper Sandusky, Ohio
&
Central Congregational Church
Madison, Ohio

CONTENTS

INTRODUCTION

I HAVE FOUND, as many people are finding, that the children's sermon can be one of the highlights—if not *the* highlight—of a worship service. Worship can be brought to life through a children's sermon—which is a special time not only for the children, but also for the adults, who are often on the edges of their pews for the only time in the service during those few minutes. Think of what can happen during the children's sermon time. There is spontaneity, enthusiasm, innocence, perhaps some laughter. These are all vital elements of worship, and yet are otherwise often missing in our services—making the children's sermon time particularly valuable.

More and more congregations are asking their pastors or other worship leaders to have children's sermons, and more and more of these persons are choosing to have them. This is so because there is the recognition that the understandings of children about God are very much formed by the relationships adults develop with the children, the time we take for them, and the lessons we endeavor to teach them. These understandings will often last their entire lives, for the saying is true, that as the twig is bent, so grows the tree.

The decision to share children's sermons on a regular basis is a good one, and yet a children's sermon every week or on any kind of a regular basis can represent a tremendous creative drain on the person responsible for them, and some creative springboard for thought can be very helpful.

I have tried to develop a book that would deal with lessons on the children's level and would inspire ideas and analogies that readers could then develop and adapt to their circumstances. All the sermons and ideas in this book have been used and well received by the children of my churches.

In beginning to make decisions about the types of sermons we will use with our children, it is necessary to have the right *goals* in mind. The goal of the children's sermon must never be to increase attendance or to be an entertainment or to impress the adults. Rather, the goal must be to communicate an understanding of God's love to the children of the church.

This happens first of all simply in the act of having children's sermons. We are taking time for the children, telling them they are special enough to call forward. A very good practice is to take a minute to introduce each child to the congregation every week by first name: "This week we have Julie, Amy, Kevin, Stevie," and so forth. If you do not know a name, ask the child. Make it a priority to learn all their names over the weeks. They are important enough to make that effort! Also, if you know a child is having a birthday or has a new hairstyle or something else special, briefly mention it as you introduce him or her.

Some other simple, practical observations may also be helpful.

- The physical setting of every sanctuary is different and offers various opportunities and restrictions for the leader to consider, but as much as possible the children should be *visible* to the congregation.
- The person-to-person contact of leader with participants is crucial. Eye contact with the children (not the adults) during this time is very important for the leader to maintain. A moderate amount of physical contact with the children can also be good.
- Another absolute necessity is to use words and examples the children can understand. The best message in the world is useless if they cannot grasp it.
- Keep the children *actively* involved. Children are naturally movers, and they associate being still with being restricted and uncomfortable. The leader who is relaxed, who walks about while talking with the children, and who allows them some freedom of

movement while they make their responses or listen to the sermon will communicate with them far more effectively.

- Allow room for *spontaneity*. Ask questions that call for *ideas*, rather than right or wrong answers. Try to get them to express their *feelings*, and always affirm every contribution with at least a nod. Have the main idea you want to communicate in mind, but avoid having the whole sermon so well rehearsed that you cannot improvise when necessary.

- Maintain a positive attitude at all times. There are no failures here, because it is a success the moment you call the children forward. You are saying, "You are important; we have time for you." The sermon may not always go exactly as planned, but that is fine. Some of the best children's sermons can come about when the children give an answer opposite to what is expected—and change the whole course of the sermon! If need be, tell them they have surprised you, and perhaps have taught you something you had not thought of before.

Included with each sermon in this book are introductory listings: the scripture reference on which the sermon is based, the object or objects required in leading the sermon discussion, and the basic concept of the sermon. These are listed for the preparation of the person who will lead the sermon. This allows him or her to know in advance what items are to be used in it, and what the basic lesson of that sermon is. In my church I have the scripture text printed in the bulletin to give the adults an opportunity for further discussion about that text at a later time in the home or classroom. Sometimes the scripture is used directly in the sermon, and sometimes it is not.

We cannot communicate God's love to the children without loving them ourselves. In the children's sermon, this love is communicated most of all by *enjoying* the time with them. There will be little positive communication if it is obvious that you are nervous with them, or that you are giving the sermon only because you feel you "should" or you "have to" have one. The leader who is able to have fun with the children, who comes into this time looking forward to it, and who has some of the same sense of wonder they have—this is the leader who will in countless ways communicate God's love, and who will enable many good things to happen in these minutes.

I hope the ideas contained in this book will serve as springboards for you in your creative processes, helping you communicate the good news of God's love to the children of your congregation and to their families.

ADVENT

A Season of Preparing

1 · Yellow-bellied Bobolinks

11/26/89

SCRIPTURE: *Mark 13:37—"And what I say to you I say to all: Watch."*

OBJECT: *A pair of binoculars*

CONCEPT: *An important part of Christmas preparation is watching.*

Good morning to all of you! This morning we're going to be starting a new group, called the Central Congregational Bird Watching Society, and I want all of you to be members! One of the things we need to have to be bird watchers is a pair of binoculars, and I have a pair right here. You know what binoculars are good for, don't you? . . . That's right, Todd; they help us see things that are far away.

I'm afraid that all I have today for our first meeting is one pair, though, so I'll have to do the watching, and I'll tell you what birds I see. *(Put binoculars to your eyes and look about.)*

Aha! There's a California quail! And over there is a tufted woodhatch! And some yellow-bellied bobolinks are

---

2

flying overhead! . . . What? Do you mean you don't believe that I can see all those birds? But you said I could see far away with my binoculars, didn't you? . . . That's right, I *can* see far away, but I can't see through the walls of the church!

If we want to be bird watchers, we have to go outside to the places where the birds might be. That's an important thing to remember. It's also important to remember that we have to watch if we want to see them.

Right now we're all starting to think about Christmas, and one of the important things to do before Christmas is to *watch*, to try to see different ways that Jesus is with us.

Do you know what? Every time we see *love*, we know that we are seeing Jesus. Does anybody have any ideas of *where* we might go to see signs of love that will help us see Jesus? What might we see that will help us become more excited and more ready for Christmas? . . . Those are all very good answers. Sunday school or regular school, wherever you are with your family or your friends—those are all places where we can see people being loving, and where we can see Jesus.

I have one other idea of a place we can look to see Jesus and his love, and that is right inside *here*—that's right, Juanita, right inside our own hearts. When we have love in our hearts, and when we love one another, then we are really getting ready for a good Christmas.

Let's stay excited as we get closer and closer to Christmas. And let's keep watching for more signs of God's love in our schools and church and homes—and in our hearts.

2 · Simon Says

SCRIPTURE: *Isaiah 40:3—"Prepare the way of the Lord."*
OBJECT: *(The game Simon Says)*
CONCEPT: *For Christians, an important part of Christmas is to prepare, to be ready, for the coming of Jesus to us.*

Have any of you ever played the game called Simon Says? It looks as though just about all of you have. How do we play this game, Deana? . . . That's right! Why don't we try to play the game right now? Simon says, "Stand up." *(Play the game for a couple of minutes, but do not draw it out to have a winner—do not eliminate anyone.)*

Okay, Simon says, "Let's all sit down and talk for a minute." What's the difference in how you are when you're playing this game? How is it different from other times, when you aren't playing? . . . Very good, Kary; it's different because we have to listen, and we have to be ready for when the leader says, "Simon says," and for when the leader doesn't.

We're lighting another candle on our Advent wreath this morning. *(It can be good to tie in each Advent children's sermon with the Advent candles and wreath and to*

---

their meaning on that day.) Today's candle reminds us to *prepare*. What does it mean to prepare, or to be prepared? . . . That's a very good answer, Cara. It means to be ready or to get ready. What do we do at Christmastime to get ready for it to come? . . . Those are all good answers. We decorate and we sing and we buy presents. We prepare ourselves.

Do you know what the most important thing to prepare is? It's our hearts. We need to be ready for Jesus to be born. We do this by looking and listening for ways that God is with us in our world, showing us love. Let's pay special attention to how people are kind and loving to one another, and be extra loving ourselves. Let's pay special attention to how pretty God has made our world this winter. And let's think about the Christmas story, and how wonderful it is that God sent Jesus to us.

I want you to remember how you paid such attention to the Simon Says game today—how you listened and were ready for each new action I suggested. Let's pay attention, and be ready just like that to see all the ways God's love is in our world, and we'll be doing what our candle says; we'll be really preparing for our Christmas celebration.

3 · Not All Spectacular: I

These "Not All Spectacular" sermons are included basically as thought starters, and are, as the title indicates, not all that spectacular. Too often we let ourselves think that every week the children's sermon must be dynamic and amazingly creative. Obviously, not every one can be. The most important thing is the relationship that is developed between the worship leader and the children from week to week in this, their special time together. The point of the "Not All Spectacular" sermons is to learn and share and grow together, discussing what is special about things that are sometimes considered common.

SCRIPTURE: *Luke 2:7—"... and laid him in a manger..."*
OBJECT: *A manger scene or picture of one*
CONCEPT: *Every part of the manger scene has a special significance.*

This is a very simple sermon, but it can be very meaningful. Simply discuss the members of the manger scene, one at a time. Allow the children to tell what they know about each person, each animal, and each object that is part of it. Then share with them some additional things, on their level, that they will also be able to understand and remember about some of the members of the scene. Encourage them to look at the manger scenes they might have at home or elsewhere, and to tell their family members and friends what they now know about that scene.

4 · *Christmas Is Hugging*

SCRIPTURE: *John 3:16—"For God so loved the world that he gave his only son . . ."*

OBJECTS: *Several strips of colored paper (enough for every child), each with a piece of tape on the end*

CONCEPT: *In sending Jesus to us, God lovingly reached out to us; now we can reach out to others and share God's love.*

Good morning to all of you! Has anybody been counting the days until Christmas? . . . That's right, Gail; there are only five days left until Christmas day—and everybody is getting more and more excited as we get closer every day!

We're going to talk about Christmas today by using these strips of paper. I want everyone to get one. Here's a green one for Duff, a blue one for Robin, a brown one for Nathan, and different colors for everybody. Now that everyone has one of these, what do you notice on the end? Very good, Dawn—there is a piece of tape on the end. With that tape, we're all going to close our pieces of paper into a circle.

But before you do that, I want you to think about what

you could do with those circles of paper. What can they make? . . . That's very good, Donald. If everyone wants to work together, you can make a *chain*. That's a good idea, but I'm leaving it up to all of you. Put your papers together however you want, okay? You may go ahead.

(The older or more outgoing children will almost certainly begin to get a couple of loops together. The chain should grow quickly from there. You may also encourage the older children to help those whose fingers are not quite able to put their loops together.)

This is beautiful! May I hold it up and show everyone what you've done? Thank you. Just look at this pretty chain!

Do you know what? Everyone had to work together and share their paper for us to make this colorful chain. We could have just kept to ourselves and made our own separate circles *(wrap your arms around yourself)*, or we could reach out to someone else, and put our papers together— sort of like a hug *(hug the child nearest you)*.

Do you know what I think? God loved the whole world so much that God wanted to reach out to hug all of us. So God sent Jesus to us on Christmas, to show this love. Now, instead of keeping to ourselves and never paying attention to anyone, we reach out to people and are kind to them and tell them about God's love. We all must work together to do this, just as we had to work together to make our chain— and then we're sharing God's gift of love with everyone.

Let's put our colorful chain on the Christmas tree in our church, as an ornament. Is that all right with you? . . . That's good, because now, every time we see it, we'll be reminded of today, and of how we learned that God loves us and sent Jesus to us because of this love. And it will also remind us that the best present we can give this Christmas—or anytime—is to share God's love with every person.

CHRISTMAS

A Season of Excitement

5 · Christmas Eve Treasure Hunt

> To Mary, then Joseph
> I first announced the story,
> And then with others in
>   my choir
> I sang of God's great glory.

SCRIPTURE: *Luke 1:26—2:20—"The time came for her to be delivered."*

OBJECTS: *(The clues below, and the many symbols in the church sanctuary, especially the manger scene)*

CONCEPT: *The Christmas story can be understood not only in learning about the various characters and objects in it, but also by the* mode *of learning about it. The excitement and discovery of this treasure-hunt experience are important parts of the Christmas message.*

How this treasure hunt is used depends entirely on the setup of the church sanctuary and the ideas of the worship leader. The presence of a manger scene, a tree and gifts, and an Advent wreath, along with the basic Christian symbols of a cross, altar candles, and so forth, are the objects or "treasures" used. The whole group can travel about the sanctuary from one stop to the next; just one child can be sent to get each clue; or the questions can simply be asked with the children allowed to guess what (or who) the answer is. Again, this is totally up to the worship leader to decide.

The clues are presented here in an order that alternates from the manger scene to other symbols, but any order can be used.

To Mary, then Joseph
I first announced the story,
And then with others in my choir
I sang of God's great glory.
   (Angel)

Because of baby Jesus' birth
The world is aglow,
For he brought to us a light
That everyone can know.
   (Altar candles)

In the history of our world
There have been many happy mothers.
But being the mother of Jesus
Brings me even more joy than others.
   (Mary)

Up in the sky I began to glow
To announce a special birth.
"Here is the town and place," I said,
"The most blessed place on earth."
   (Star)

We count the weeks till Christmas—
Four weeks, three, then two.
We plan for Jesus' birthday,
Lighting a candle that's new.
   (Advent wreath)

Some say I am a humble place,
Not a very nice place to roam.
But I will always proudly say,
"I was baby Jesus' first home."
   (Manger)

Like Jesus who lives forever,
I show you a living scene.
You bring me in at Christmas,
Because I'm always green.
(Tree)

Angels appeared at night to us,
Singing with great joy,
Telling us the wondrous news—
The birth of a baby boy.
(Shepherds)

Without a car
We traveled far.
We followed that star—
And now here we are!
(Wise men)

Because of that great love
Shown by the wise men three,
You, too, will find a few of us
This year underneath your tree.
(Gifts)

There are many celebrations at Christmastime,
With parties and gifts and trees that are tall.
But I hope that through this you find meaning
By celebrating my birth most of all.
(Jesus)

The above clues may be reproduced for use in local churches.

6 · *Gifts of Joy*

SCRIPTURE: *1 Chronicles 29:17—"I have seen thy people
. . . offering freely and joyously . . ."*
OBJECT: *A simple gift for each child*
CONCEPT: *We find great joy in giving to others because God
has given to us.*

I know that all of you have received special gifts for Christmas. Am I right? . . . Good, I'm glad. Have any of you *given*
some special presents to your mom or dad or to a friend this
year? . . . Good! I'm glad to hear that too.

How does it make you feel when you have given a
present? . . . Samantha says it makes her feel very happy.
That's something important to remember.

I have presents to share with all of you this morning.
These were all made by Mrs. Gillespie, and she has asked
me to give one to each of you. You may each pick out the
color you want, and while you do, we'll talk a little bit
more.

Why do you think Mrs. Gillespie would take the time
and go to all the work to make these, and then give them all
away to you? . . . Rachel? . . . That's right—for the same

15

reason that we said before. It makes her happy. It makes people happy to be able to give presents.

At Christmastime we are very happy because of the birth of Jesus. Jesus is a gift to us from God, a gift that makes us happier than anything else. The gift of Jesus makes us so happy that we want to share our happiness with others. That's why we give presents at Christmas.

There's a special feeling that comes to us when we give to others, whether it's at Christmas or at some other time.

God loves us and we love each other. That's why we have these gifts to share today, and why we give to each other at other times. Whenever you give a present to someone else and it makes you feel very happy, remember that it is God's love that helps you feel that way.

EPIPHANY

A Season of Sharing

7 · *Not All Spectacular: II*

12/31/89 AO

SCRIPTURE: *Matthew 2:11—"Then, opening their trea-sures, they offered him gifts."*
OBJECT: *Something you received as a Christmas present*
CONCEPT: *There is a very special reason why we give and receive Christmas gifts.*

This lesson consists simply of asking the children what special gifts they received for Christmas. It may be a good idea to limit each child to telling briefly about one gift that was special. This will keep the discussion from becoming too concerned about quantities of presents, and should prevent the children from comparing their quantities. The point of your questions should be to get them to share their excitement and joy over a particular gift.

After the children have each had a turn, it is important for you to share with them something that was particularly meaningful for you in your gifts this year.

Finally, and most importantly, ask the children why it is that we started giving gifts at Christmas in the first place, and lead into a brief discussion about the wise men, and how our reasons are the same as theirs were—the joy we have over God's gift of Jesus.

If Santa is mentioned by the children in this time, as he may well be, try to bring out the positive aspects that can be seen in his giving without receiving in return.

8 · Love in the Rocks

A.D. Jan 89

SCRIPTURE: *Genesis 1:20—"And God said, 'Let the waters bring forth swarms of living creatures.'"*
OBJECTS: *Water and ice*
CONCEPT: *God has put properties into the natural world that show great love for all creatures.*

Do you know what a miracle is? Who can tell me? . . . Earl? . . . Very good. A miracle is something—a good thing—that isn't supposed to happen. Often, we think of miracles as things that go against the usual laws of nature.

But do you know what? I think that there are some pretty great miracles right in the regular way that God made our world of nature. I want to show you a miracle right now, by dropping these two ice cubes into this glass of water.

Look at that! Do you see a miracle? . . . Michael says nothing unusual happened. That's right. Nothing ususual happened. But what *did* happen? . . . Yes, Todd, very good. The ice cubes floated to the top. *That* is a miracle—and I'll tell you why.

When water is getting colder and colder, and is almost

cold enough to freeze, a strange thing happens. The water starts to expand. That means it gets a little bit bigger.

When the men in our Men's Club make apple cider, they always freeze some to save for later in the year. Before they freeze it, though, they have to pour some of it out of each jug. The water in it will get bigger when it is frozen, and if they don't pour some of it out to make room, it will burst the container!

Nobody, not even scientists, can explain exactly why water does this. But they do know that it is very important. It's important because that makes it get lighter, and come to the top of the water.

Right now our lake and our ponds are all frozen over on top. But underneath the ice that has risen to the top, all the fish and other sea life are able to live and find food.

This is truly a miracle, because it allows our fish and other sea life to live through the icy winters. It is a miracle because our God of love cares for them and made it to be this way.

The next time you see ice in a cold drink, floating on the top, remember what a miracle that is. Remember the God of love who created that miracle.

9 · *The Candy Man*

SCRIPTURE: *1 John 4:19—"We love, because [God] first loved us."*

OBJECTS: *A candy dispenser in the shape of a man (available at most dime or drug stores) with five or six candies in it, and a packet of refills*

CONCEPT: *For people to share love, they need also to have love shared with them.*

This morning is such a special morning, and I've brought a friend of mine to be with us. Have you ever seen one of these before? . . . That's right, Becky; this is a candy man. What does this toy do? . . . Very good, Jeff—he gives candy to us.

Why don't we let him give a piece of candy to each of us? Here, Matt, you may have one. And Lynn, here is one for you to take. Isn't this wonderful? This candy man just keeps giving more and more candy to all of us! Here is another for Linnette, and another for Jill.

Hey! What happened here? Why isn't the candy man giving any more candy to us? Mark, what do you think? . . .

I think you're right. He can't give any more because he ran out. Look—he's empty inside!

Well, it so happens that I have a refill pack here in my pocket, and we'll help this toy fill up with candy again. *(While you are putting the refills in, make the following explanation.)* Do you know what? This reminds me of how *people* are. Sometimes a person gives and gives to help other people until the person just gets worn out and empty. And every person needs to be filled up again, just like this candy man.

And do you know how we help fill people up again? Do you have any ideas? . . . That's right, Fred; we help fill people by being kind and loving to them. God has given us love, and now we share it with others and help them be filled with love. Then they are so full of love that they can share it with someone else, and that love just keeps going and going.

Sometimes we think that our moms and dads and teachers should be able just to keep giving and giving forever. But let's remember that they get "empty" sometimes too, just like our candy man, and they need our love to help fill them again.

Look! Our candy man is all full and happy again, and now he can share a piece of candy with everyone who didn't get one yet! He's glad that we helped him to be full again—and so are we!

10 · *Orange Trees in Ohio*

SCRIPTURE: *Genesis 1:11-12—"Let the earth put forth vege-tation . . . fruit trees bearing fruit in which is their seed, each according to its kind."*

OBJECT: *Something that does not grow in your region's climate*

CONCEPT: *Different parts of the world have various kinds of weather, and this allows all the different things we need to be grown and made.*

Good morning, my friends—and it *is* a good morning. Do you know what I did the first thing this morning? Well, I went out to our backyard, walked over to our orange tree, and picked a couple of oranges for breakfast! Here are a couple of extras I picked. Aren't they beautiful?

. . . Wait a minute! What's that? Melissa says she doesn't believe me! Do you mean you don't think I picked these from our orange tree? You don't even believe we *have* an orange tree?

Well, you're right. I have to admit I was just trying to fool you. These oranges didn't come from our yard. Do you know where they *did* come from? . . . That's right; they came from a real orange tree. . . . Very good, Linda—they came from an orange tree in Florida.

You knew that we just came back from a trip to Florida, didn't you? While we were there we saw palm trees; we saw banana and orange and grapefruit trees. None of these things grow in Ohio, do they? Why don't they? . . . That's right, Jennifer; it gets too cold here. That snow we have wouldn't be very good for an orange tree.

But do you know what? Many things grow in Ohio that I never saw in Florida. We grow wheat and corn and beans here; we raise more animals here. I didn't see some of the things in Florida that we have here.

All over the world people have different kinds of weather, and different things grow in each place. If all the world had weather like Ohio, or if all the world had weather like Florida, that wouldn't be good, because then some things couldn't be grown anywhere.

But God loves us so much that God made different kinds of weather all over. Each place grows different things, and then we share what we've grown and made. The next time you eat an orange, think of how our friends in Florida grew it for us. The next time you see one of our fields, think of how we're growing things to share with other people. And always remember how much God loves us—giving us different kinds of weather—so we can grow and share our different crops.

11 · Counting a Snowball

SCRIPTURE: *1 Corinthians 12:27—"Now you are the body of Christ and individually members of it."*
OBJECTS: *Scissors and a sheet of paper*
CONCEPT: *Each of us is unique and special, but we can join together to do very important parts of God's work.*

What do you think of all the snow we've had this week? Isn't it amazing? What are some things we can do in the snow? . . . Very good. Those are all things that I like too.

Have you ever wondered how many snowflakes are out there right now? Let's think about that for a minute. How many snowflakes do you think are piled by the side of the walk where Mr. Nash shoveled them? Or how many do you think there are in a snowman or a snowball? What do you think? . . .

Douglas says a hundred. . . . Tessa says a thousand. . . . You say a million? Maybe . . . maybe that many and even more just in one snowball or snowman.

And do you know what? Every single one of those hundreds and thousands and millions of snowflakes is different! That's right! No two are alike. Isn't that amazing, that God would make every snowflake to be a little different from all the others?

I remember that when I was in school we used to fold a piece of paper and cut little corners and holes out of it to make a snowflake. Have you ever done that? . . . While we talk some more, I'm going to try to make one.

What I want us to remember today is how special each snowflake is—different from all the others. And I want us to remember how all those snowflakes together can do such amazing things. They can make snowballs and snow forts. They can work together so we can go sledding on top of them. They can even pile up so high that cars and trucks can't drive through them.

All of this reminds me of how God loves us and has made each one of us to be different from anyone else. And it also reminds me of how all of us, working together through God's church, can do very big and special things. We sing and worship. We help the family we sponsor. We send gifts to people who are in need. Those are some of the special things that happen when we work together.

Look! My snowflake is done! Let's see how it looks. Say, it's not too bad! It isn't as pretty as the ones that God makes, but I still like it.

Maybe you can do this at home later today. And maybe it will remind you of what we talked about this morning. Whenever you're playing in the snow, think about how God made each snowflake in a special way, and how God made each one of us in a special way. And think about all the things we're able to do when we work together.

12 · The Giving Tray

SCRIPTURE: *2 Corinthians 9:7-8—"God loves a cheerful giver. And God is able to provide you with every blessing in abundance."*

OBJECT: *A clear ice-cube tray with colored water in all but one of its sections*

CONCEPT: *When many share, it makes a tremendous difference for one who is in need.*

Today at our church we're going to have a special offering. Did any of you hear me talking about that already this morning? Good! I'm sure many of your parents are going to help by giving to this offering. I want us to learn why we have these offerings, and what they do, so you'll be able to understand them better whenever you hear me talking about them from now on.

To help us learn, we're going to use this. . . . That's right, Alex; it's an ice-cube tray. Now, look in it and tell me what you see. . . . That's right! I have blue water in it. I want you to know that usually I don't use blue water to make ice cubes. They would look pretty funny in my lemonade.

Today we're using blue water, though, so you'll be able

to see it better and understand what we're doing. Who can count well enough to tell everyone how many ice cubes we're going to make? Karyn . . . Very good, we'll have thirteen ice cubes, because thirteen of the squares have water in them. That's right, Bobbie; there's one square that's empty, and it won't have an ice cube.

But if I take the tray like this, and tip it just a little— look what's happening! Now how many ice cubes will there be? . . . Nikki says now we have fourteen, instead of thir- teen—and she's right, isn't she? A little bit of water from each square ran down into the empty square and filled it up, and we can't even tell that any of the others are any different from before.

When we have special offerings in church, it's like this ice-cube tray. Each of us has been given much by God, so we all share some of it. Even then we still have plenty, and the people who are in need, like the empty ice-cube section, are helped very much by what we give. They may be able to buy food or clothes; they may be able to go to a doctor, if there is someone in their family who is sick; or they may be able to go to school—using the money they are given from our offering.

Like the ice-cube trays, filling the empty section, we each give something to help the people in our world who are in need.

LENT

A Season of Learning

13 · My Apple Divided for You

SCRIPTURE: *1 Corinthians 11:24—"And when he had given thanks, he broke it . . ."*

OBJECT: *An apple*

CONCEPT: *We feel especially close to Christ, and to each other, when we share a portion of food.*

A little bit later in our worship service we are going to have Holy Communion. Most of your parents will be taking communion, and some of you even have brothers or sisters who will be taking it.

I remember when I was your age I used to be unhappy on communion Sundays. I was unhappy because I wasn't old enough to be allowed to have communion. I didn't like it that my parents and other people were having something to eat and doing something special without me! Have any of you ever felt that way? Maybe you don't understand what is happening in communion, or why you can't have it, too? . . . Do you? I thought you might, so today I thought I'd talk with you a little bit about communion.

We know that Jesus died on a cross and then came back to life. And we also know that Jesus had done nothing wrong, and did not deserve to die. Yet, he was willing to die for us because he loved us so much.

The last time that Jesus ate with his disciples, he wanted to be sure that they understood how important this was—how he was giving his life for us.

Jesus wanted to be sure we would always be reminded of what he was going to do, so he told his disciples that whenever they were eating together they should remember him and feel close to him. Then Jesus took a loaf of bread and broke it into pieces for them to eat, as a way for them to be reminded of what he was doing.

When we take communion we're doing what Jesus asked us to remember to do. Do you see the bread? All of us will eat a piece of bread that comes from the same loaf, to show we are all together in remembering what Jesus has done for us. When we do this, we feel close to Jesus, and close to each other.

Do you have questions about any of this? . . .

I'm glad for how you have listened and for the questions you have asked. As you continue to grow up, I hope that you'll continue to learn more about communion. In your Sunday school and confirmation classes, you'll learn more about it, so that when you're old enough to participate, you'll understand it, and it will be special to you.

This talk we've had has been very special to me. To remember it, I want us to do a little bit of what Jesus did, only we'll use an apple. Let's see, there are fourteen of us, so I'll cut this apple into fourteen pieces. . . . Now I want each of you to take a piece to eat. . . . Now we have all shared a part of the same apple. That helps me to feel even closer to all of you, and will help me to remember the special talk we've just had.

There is much more to communion than just what we've talked about today, but sharing something to eat and feeling close together is part of God's love in Jesus that we remember whenever we have communion.

14 · Lifting Up

SCRIPTURE: *Psalm 121:2—"My help comes from [God], who made heaven and earth."*

OBJECT: *A pair of glasses, a cane, or some other such item that is an aid to people*

CONCEPT: *We are thankful to God for things that help people to overcome handicaps.*

Have any of you noticed anything different about me this morning? . . . It looks as though most of you have! Yes, Steven, that's right. I am wearing glasses. I just got them this past week. The eye doctor says that I should wear them when I am reading or driving. Gayle and Jeff and Barbie all have glasses, and now I do too.

Glasses help people, and I'm glad. I'm glad I have mine, because they help me to see so much better. What are some other things that help people the way glasses do? Can you think of any other things? . . . Yes, hearing aids . . . canes . . . wheelchairs. These are all things that help people to see or hear better, or to get around better.

I've been wondering something all week, though, and I want to ask you about what I've been thinking. I've been wondering why God has made us so that sometimes we need glasses or a cane or one of these other things. Why didn't God just make every one of us perfect, so that we would never need any of these things? What do you think? . . . Any ideas at all. . . . Yes, Todd . . . You're right. That is a hard question—a very hard question. It's one that we really cannot answer, can we?

I certainly don't know the answer to my question. But I do know that I'm glad God has helped people to discover ways to help one another. I'm glad because I know that God cares for us, and God wants us to care for each other.

There are many things that happen that we can't explain, many things that happen that we wish would not happen. We don't understand everything. But we do understand that God loves us. And we also know how much happier we are when we help care for one another.

Whenever you see a pair of glasses or a cane or something else like this, I hope you will think about how glad we are that God has helped us to make these things that help people. We're glad because God cares for us—just as we are—and God wants us to care for one another.

15 · Bits and Pieces

SCRIPTURE: *Deuteronomy 4:44—"This is the law which Moses set before the children of Israel."*

OBJECTS: *Fresh fruit and pieces of the same fruit, dried*

CONCEPT: *God has given us minds that are able to remember the essence of the lessons and experiences of our lives.*

Most of you go to school now, and I've heard that you have many things to learn and remember in school. Is this true? . . . What are some of the things you have to remember? . . . The times tables . . . the stories you've been reading . . . how to read . . . what time to go to school . . . all the names of the other children in your class.

Those are many, many things to remember, and I know those are just a few of the things you have to remember, aren't they?

I've been thinking about this. Do you remember everything from school? I mean, do you remember every word that you read, and every word your teacher says? . . . No, of course not. You can't remember everything. But you can remember the most important things.

The same is true when we learn about the Bible. The

Bible is very big, with many stories and lessons in it. Nobody can remember every word from it; but we can remember what is most important from it.

To help you think more about this, I want to have you think about this—this banana. What would happen if I decided I didn't want to eat this banana today, but wanted to save it? How many days could I wait and have it still be good? . . . Yes, Jill, I would say just two or three more days, and then this banana won't be good any more.

But we can still save the important part of this banana for a long time. Look at this jar. In it are what we call banana chips. We make them by cutting a banana into slices and putting them into a food dryer. The food dryer blows hot air onto the banana slices and dries them out. All the moisture, all the parts of the banana that might spoil, are taken away. But the important part of the banana is left.

It's a small amount that is left. As a matter of fact, a big banana like this will only make a stack of banana chips a couple of inches high. It probably took nine or ten bananas to fill this one jar with banana chips.

But the essence—that is, the important part—is all left. Most of what is good for us in bananas is left in the chips, and after we've put them into a jar we can save them for a long, long time.

What's that, Matt? . . . You've always wondered what these taste like? Well, I'm glad, because I think you should all try a few right now for a snack. . .

Now, I want you to think about how God has made us with very special minds. We don't remember everything, but we remember most important things—just as the banana chip has most of the important parts of the banana. God has given us minds that can remember the important lessons at school, or from our Bibles, or the other things we do each day.

From now on, whenever you eat a dried banana or apple, or a raisin that is made from a grape, or some other dried fruit, I hope it will remind you of our lesson today. Remember how much God loves you, that you have the special mind that you do.

---

16 · Behind the Back

2/5/89 A.O.

SCRIPTURE: *Joshua 24:15—"Choose this day whom you will serve."*

OBJECTS: *Enough pieces of candy or gum for all the children*

CONCEPT: *We are given freedom to make choices, and God gives us guidance to make the best ones we can.*

This morning we're going to play a game I'm sure you've played before. It's called Guess Which Hand? or Behind the Back. Someone puts their hands behind their back and puts something into one of them; then, if you guess which hand has it, you get to keep it.

I have some gum here—don't worry, parents, it's sugarless! I hope many of you will win a piece for yourselves by guessing which of my hands has it.

There's only going to be one difference today from the way this game is usually played. Before you guess which hand, I want you to watch to see if there is any *clue* for you about which hand is the correct one to choose.

Okay, Albert, let's start with you, and watch carefully! *(As you bring your hands out, give a clue, such as a*

---

wiggling thumb or moving the correct hand up and down, so they will know which one to choose. As each child chooses correctly—as they all should—praise him or her aloud. This process can become rather lengthy; if you usually have fifteen or more children at a sermon, it would be wise to have someone, such as one of your youth fellowship members, help you by playing the game with some of the children.)

That was really fun, wasn't it? Every one of you won! Do you know what? We all made the right choices, because we all had clues—but no one *had* to choose what they did.

This is very much like our lives, because God gives us clues too, in the Bible and in the answering of our prayers, and in the help our parents and teachers give us. God gives us clues about how to make the best choices in our lives. Nobody *has* to choose what God says, because we're free to make up our own minds. But God gives us clues about how to choose, because God wants us to have good things and happy lives.

It would have been much harder to pick the correct hand today if you didn't get clues, wouldn't it? But I *wanted* you to choose the hand with the gum, because that's a good thing. And God wants all of us to have good things in our lives—so let's always listen for the ways God gives us clues for living the best ways, and try our best to follow those clues.

17 · Riddles and Parables

SCRIPTURE: *Luke 13:18-19—". . . It is like a grain of mustard seed. . . ."*

OBJECTS: *Some riddles and a seed*

CONCEPT: *Some of Jesus' teachings are hard to understand at first. They are like riddles that make us think—and help us enjoy our thinking!*

One of the basic teachings of Jesus was about the kingdom of God. The term "kingdom" is no longer a common one in our language, however, and the idea of the kingdom is an especially difficult one for children to understand without some further—and simpler—clarification.

We have taken the liberty here of substituting the idea of God's love and its growth within and among us in place of the term "kingdom." Each person using this sermon is free to use this or any other adaptation that he or she finds helpful.

"Riddles and Parables" is a basic approach that can be used with children in beginning to interpret many of Jesus' parables.

How many of you like riddles? . . . That's good, because I do, too, and I'm going to ask you some today. Here's the first one. How do we know that a train can hear? . . . Because it has engineers! Here's another. When is a giant little? . . . When he is with his big sister! Now, here is one more. What is the hardest thing about learning to roller skate? . . . The sidewalk!

Do any of you have a riddle you would like to ask? . . . Okay, Glen, how about you? . . .

Riddles are fun to ask, and fun to guess, aren't they? They are fun because they make us think. Do you know what? Jesus liked to tell riddles to people too, because he liked to have fun, and he liked to get people to think. He told parables, and some of them are like our riddles.

One time Jesus said that the love of God is like a seed. And everyone wondered what he meant by that. So they all started to think about what he had said, to try to understand what he meant.

Do you know what this is? . . . That's right, Ricky; it's a seed. It's an apple seed. Have any of you ever seen an apple tree? . . . Just about all of you have. If we plant this seed in the ground, what will happen? . . . Very good, Duane. It will grow into an apple tree. But an apple tree is so big, and this seed is so little. How can this happen? . . . Of course—God makes it grow.

Some people thought about Jesus' riddle, and they began to figure out what he meant. A seed is little, but it grows into something big. In our hearts, we may have just a little bit of God's love, about as little as this seed. But God makes it grow. God makes it become big! And what wonderful, big things we can do because of God's love in our hearts!

From now on, whenever we hear a riddle that makes us think, let's remember that Jesus liked to have fun telling riddles too, and he liked to make people think. And whenever we see a seed, let's think about how it can grow into something big, just as God's love inside us can grow into something big.

18 · Invisible Made Visible

SCRIPTURE: *John 3:8—"The wind blows where it wills, and you hear the sound of it, but you do not know whence it comes or whither it goes."*

OBJECTS: *A small wastebasket and several strips of paper, about three inches by one inch*

CONCEPT: *Though we cannot see God, we can see what God does, and we know God is with us.*

I have some old pieces of paper here this morning, and I'm all through using them now. I don't need them any more. What should I do with them, now that I'm finished with them? . . .

That's right, Krissy. I should throw them away. I shouldn't throw them in the street or in the park or on someone's lawn, because we don't want to litter. No, I should throw them into a wastebasket—and what a lucky thing! There just happens to be a wastebasket right over here, under this pew!

That is lucky! I'll just bring this wastebasket out here, and I'll drop my papers into it. *(Hold a paper about two feet above the basket and let it drop.)* What's happening here? I dropped my paper, but it didn't go into the basket. Everyone watch, to be sure I'm holding the paper right above the wastebasket, and I'll try again. . . . Oh, my, that one didn't work, either. *(Let some of the children try. Most of them should also "miss.")*

What do you think is happening? Why do the papers float to the side, instead of dropping straight in? . . .

What, Dennis? The air makes it move? I don't see any air between here and the basket. Do any of you see air in here? . . . That's right, Bernard; we can't see it, but we still know it's here, because we can see what it does. We know the air is here because we're breathing it, and it keeps us alive. When we drop a paper and it moves, we can tell there is air that makes it move.

Did any of you ever hear your parents or your Sunday school teachers or someone else say that God is a Spirit? Well, that's a word that is hard to understand, but it's a little bit like the air in this room. We can't see it, but we know it's here, because we breathe it and we see what it does.

In the same sort of way, God is a Spirit. That means that God is invisible. We can't see God, but we can see what God does. We can see the beautiful world God has made; we see our friends and our family that God loves and helps us love. We know that every time we breathe, God is giving us that breath of life.

Remember how the paper moves, even though we don't see the air that makes it move. And remember that even though we cannot see God—since God is a Spirit—we still know God is here, because we can see what God does.

HOLY WEEK

A Season of Pondering

19 · Follow-ups: I

A "follow-up" children's sermon takes place in parts over two or more sessions. Such extended sermons are especially effective because each additional lesson reinforces the original concept. Of course, if the group of children varies considerably from week to week, then you may not want to use this approach. In any case, each lesson should be self-contained. Each additional lesson must add a new angle or understanding to the whole picture or pattern being developed.

SCRIPTURE: *1 Corinthians 15:35-36—"How are the dead raised? . . . What you sow does not come to life unless it dies."*

OBJECTS: *Any kind of seed or seeds, and a pot of dirt in which to plant them*

CONCEPT: *We see the miracle of the resurrection of Jesus all around us—in the ways that seeds grow to new life.*

This sermon is very basic—one you may have considered already. It parallels the miracle of a seed's sprouting through the ground with the miracle of the resurrection of Jesus. Allow the children to talk about what they know about seeds; allow them to help plant the seeds you have in appropriately sized pots. Then talk to them about what they expect will happen to those seeds in the coming week, and draw some parallels from that with the miracle God showed us in the resurrection.

The follow-up comes when you gather the children a week or so later, and have them look at the little sprouts that have come through the dirt. Discussion on the fulfillment of God's promises, and further discussion on the resurrection, can come from this follow-up session. It can be especially meaningful to plant the seeds at the beginning of Holy Week, so that they will be visibly sprouting on Easter morning.

One other positive aspect of this follow-up sermon is that if the pots are kept in a specific area of the sanctuary or a classroom, it can add to the children's feeling of having a special place where they gather for their sermons.

20 · There's No Stopping It!

SCRIPTURE: *Matthew 27:66—"So they went and made the sepulchre secure by sealing the stone and setting a guard."*

OBJECTS: *Some winter play items*

CONCEPT: *Because God wanted Jesus to come back to life, it was sure to happen.*

I want to talk to you this morning about having fun in the winter. I like playing games and doing things outdoors in the wintertime. Do you too? Good. Tell me, what are some things that you like to do outdoors in the winter? . . . Those are all good things, and I like to do them too.

I've brought some things to show you today. These are my mittens that I've used to make hundreds of snowballs, and this is my sled that I've had so much fun riding down big hills. I've had so much fun this winter, but now I'm afraid that winter may be ending, and I don't want it to. As a matter of fact, I've even seen some robins lately, and people tell me that robins are a sure sign that winter is

---

ending and spring is coming. Have any of you seen any robins lately? . . . T.J. has, and so has Kim. . . . Yes, many of you have.

Well, I've come up with a great plan that will keep spring from coming. Every time I see a robin, I'm going to chase it away! I'm going to shout, "Go back South until next month!" Then, when I've chased all the robins away, that will keep spring from coming so soon. Don't you think that's a good idea?

. . . What? Christie doesn't think it's a very good idea. Why not? Why won't it work? . . . I see. . . . That's right. First of all, I never could chase all the robins away, could I? And even if I could, that wouldn't keep spring from coming. It is sure to come because God wants it to come. God wants us to have fun in the nice spring weather, just as we've had fun in the winter weather.

Do you know what this reminds me of? This reminds me of the verse in the Bible that tells us that some people did not want Jesus to come back to life after he died on the cross. So, while he was in the tomb, they put a big stone in front of it to keep him from coming back.

But that was silly—just as silly as trying to keep spring from coming by chasing robins. Jesus was sure to come back to life because God loves us.

In the days ahead, when we're playing outdoors and enjoying the spring weather, let's remember that spring comes because God wants it to, just as Jesus came back to life because God wanted him to.

EASTERTIDE

A Season of Special Feelings

21 · Not All Spectacular: III

SCRIPTURE: *Matthew 28:8—"They departed quickly from the tomb with fear and great joy. . . ."*

OBJECTS: *Colored eggs, baskets, or other decorations of the Easter season*

CONCEPT: *There is a reason why we do some of the special things we do on Easter: it is our joy after learning of Jesus' resurrection.*

This is a very open-ended sermon, depending largely on the customs or traditions in your community and church. Talk to the children about what has happened this Easter morning in their homes or at Sunday school or at another church function. Have they been exciting things?

Then simply talk to them about why we do these different things—how the colored eggs remind us of the new life of Jesus after he was raised from death, how the excitement we have when we find an egg reminds us of how excited the disciples were when they learned that Jesus was alive. Affirm all the activities the children share that are exciting and special to them at Easter. And point in each case to the joy we feel on Easter, and to how special we are to God, that God would show such love for us through Jesus. These things make all our celebrations possible and meaningful.

Other "Not All Spectacular" sermons can be done at many times of the year, particularly on holidays, by talking about what things we do and why it is we do them. This is modeled after the Passover custom in which the children ask, "Why is this night different from all other nights?"

22 · *Really Special*

SCRIPTURE: *Matthew 10:30—"But even the hairs of your head are all numbered."*

OBJECT: *Something that is of great sentimental value to you— though not worth very much monetarily*

CONCEPT: *We matter much more than anyone can fully understand—because God loves us so much.*

Who can tell me what season is starting now? . . . That's right; it's the spring season. What other season begins in the spring? . . . Very good, Jackie—baseball season starts now!

I want to take something out of this bag and show it to you. It's something very special to me. You can see that it's a baseball glove, and it's pretty old and worn, isn't it? This glove is very special to me because my father gave it to me when I was in the third grade. Is anyone here in the third grade? . . . Brian is. Ever since I was as old as Brian, I have had this glove. And all these years it's been my favorite one, even though it's become quite old and worn out.

Do you know what? If someone today said they would give me $100 for this glove, I wouldn't take it! Do you know why? . . . That's right, Kristin, it isn't worth that much money! So why do you think I wouldn't take that much for this glove if I had the chance? . . . That's exactly right. It's because this is a very special glove to me, one that my father gave me a long time ago, and I could never buy another one that would mean so much to me. Even $100— or any amount of money—could not mean the same to me, because this glove is so special.

There's something else I want to tell you today too. That is that every one of us is worth more to God than we could ever explain or understand. God loves every one of us. We're all really special to God, and nothing could ever replace any of us. The Bible tells us that God knows everything about each one of us. Look at Beth's hair. The Bible says that God even knows how many hairs we have. God knows how we feel when we're happy or when we're sad. God knows what we hope to do someday, and what we like doing today.

My baseball glove is special because when I see it and put it on, I think about all the fun I've had playing with it, and about some of the games I've played with it. I remember how happy I was when my dad first gave it to me.

It reminds me of how we're all really special to God, because God made us and God loves us just the way we are.

23 · *Brenda Pringle*

SCRIPTURE: *Deuteronomy 7:6—"God has chosen you to be a people . . ."*

OBJECT: *A can of Pringle's potato chips*

CONCEPT: *We are thankful that God has made each of us different and special.*

Good morning to all of you! I'll bet most of you have seen one of these before, and can tell me exactly what it is. . . . That's right! It's a can of Pringle's potato chips. Maybe some of you haven't tried them before, and maybe some of you already like them.

I'm going to give each of you one of these this morning and ask you to hold it up for everyone to see. If you can't resist, you can eat it now, or you can wait until later. As I give you your chip, I'm going to give each of you a new name.

Here you are. Today you aren't Lindsay, you're Lindsay Pringle. You are Shannon Pringle, and you are Ryan Pringle. Today I'm Harold Pringle. Now, as we hold our Pringle's potato chips up, what do we notice about them? . . . That's right! They are all exactly the same! If Jimmy and Andy traded, we'd have a hard time telling which was which.

Many people think it's pretty great that Pringle's

---

potato chips are all alike, because they fit into this can so nicely, and their commercials tell us how they are so perfect.

What do you think of this? Do you like being Pringles? . . . I think you're right. It's fine for potato chips all to look the same, but I'm glad we aren't like that. I'm glad that we aren't really Gary Pringle or Starlena Pringle, and all look the same.

When God made us, God wanted each of us to be special, so God made every one of us different from the other. I know who each of you is when I see you, because you all look different. You all have different things that you like to have and different things you like to do.

Let's be extra thankful today that God didn't make us all alike. God loves us and wants each one of us to be special, so God made each one of us different from anyone else in the world. The way we are all special and different is one of the gifts of God's love.

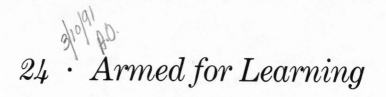

24 · *Armed for Learning*

SCRIPTURE: *Acts 1:8—"And you shall be my witnesses in Jerusalem and in all Judea and Samaria and to the end of the earth."*

OBJECTS: *(The children themselves)*

CONCEPT: *We learn and use many different things as we share God's love with others.*

Last week I had a chance to visit with a missionary. Can anybody here tell me what a missionary does? . . . Hmmm . . . Well, sort of. Can anybody tell me something more about a missionary? . . . Yes, very good, Matt. A missionary is someone who goes to another land to help people in different ways, in order to share God's love.

Some missionaries are doctors or nurses. Some are ministers or builders. And some are schoolteachers. The missionary I visited is a teacher in a school in South America. Teaching the children how to read and write is her way of helping others and showing God's love.

This teacher told me that they have one problem in their school, and do you know what it is? Their problem is that they don't always know when the children are old enough to start school. . . . That's right. That's hard for us to understand, but sometimes people in other lands aren't able to write down birthdays and remember them as well as we do. My missionary friend tells me that so many children want to come to the school to learn to read and write, and sometimes children are not really old enough for school yet when they come. It would be better for these children to wait until they are old enough—but nobody knows for sure how old each child is.

So do you know what my friend the missionary does? Let me show you. I'll need some volunteers. How about Michelle, and Eathan, and Corey. What I want you to do is to reach your arm over your head and try to touch your ear on the other side of your head. This is how the missionary teacher tells when children are old enough to start school!

Look! Michelle can do it easily. Michelle, you're in the third grade, aren't you? It's easy to see that you are old enough for school. Look at Eathan. He can't reach because he's still too young for school. Oh, look at Corey! Corey can reach his ear, but I don't think he's putting his arm right over the top of his head. Let's try it that way. . . . See, now Corey can almost reach, but not quite. Corey will be ready for school next year, won't you, Corey?

My missionary friend tells me they have learned that God makes our bodies grow in such a way that we can do this—we can reach our arm over our head and touch our ear—just at the time that we're old enough to start school. So even when missionaries don't know how old the children are, they are still able to do this to see which ones are old enough for school.

I hope you'll remember this. Maybe you can try it with some of your friends, or your brothers and sisters, and tell them that this is how missionaries know which children are old enough to start school.

I hope that you'll remember that missionaries help other people and show God's love to them.

25 · *Rosy Medicine*

Summer 91 A.O.

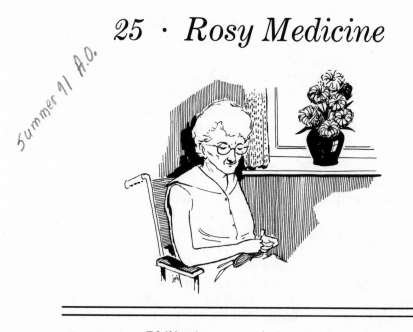

SCRIPTURE: *Philippians 4:18—"I am filled, having received . . . the gifts you sent, a fragrant offering."*
OBJECTS: *The altar flowers*
CONCEPT: *Through the beauty of our expressions of concern, people are given healing strength.*

Right behind us, next to our altar, are beautiful flowers, given to our church by Mr. and Mrs. Boerner in memory of people they've loved in their family. Mr. and Mrs. Boerner have told me that after our worship I may take these flowers to someone in our church who is in the hospital.

This reminds me of a day not long ago when I was visiting a woman who was in the hospital. There in her room were some flowers that someone from our church had brought to her. And do you know what she said to me? She said those flowers had helped her to feel better and better.

Now, I don't understand that at all, do you? I mean, I've been looking at these flowers very carefully, and I don't see any medicine or anything else in there that would help someone to get better. So, how could these flowers help someone in the hospital? Do you have any idea? . . .

Yes, Suzanne, they are very pretty, and they smell nice too. That's very important, because pretty things from God's world help us to feel better. . . . Colleen? Yes, that's another reason. And it's a very important one. The flowers help the woman in the hospital because they make her think of her friends who brought them to her. Every time she looks at them, they remind her that her friends at the church love her and are thinking of her and praying for her.

God has made us in such a way that we get stronger and healthier just by seeing and smelling beautiful things. God has also made us in such a way that we feel better, and often grow healthier, when we know that people care about us.

That's why flowers are such nice presents to give to someone—especially someone who hasn't been feeling well or who has been sad about something. It's a kind, caring thing to do.

I hope you'll remember this, and think of more things you can do for others. It will help us have a more caring world—and a healthier and happier world, too.

26 · Watering What We Do Not See

SCRIPTURE: *Matthew 23:26—"First cleanse the inside of the cup and of the plate, that the outside also may be clean."*

OBJECTS: *A house plant and a spray bottle of water*

CONCEPT: *Though the outward appearance of a plant or of a person is important, it is the health and beauty of what we do not see that matters most.*

How many of you have plants in your house? . . . Good, just about everybody does. We do too, and I brought one of ours over to show you this morning.

This is a snake plant, and it is a very pretty plant. It's especially pretty when its leaves are moist and shiny.

I have here a spray bottle, filled with water. This is used for putting a light mist of water on plants, and that helps them to be pretty and healthy. Would any of you like to help me by spraying some water on the leaves of my plant? Good . . . thank you, Jennifer. . . . Now, Joshua, it's your turn. . . .

That was very good. Look how shiny and pretty our plant looks now!

But I have a question to ask you. What would happen if I sprayed my plant's leaves like this every day, but this was all the water I ever gave it? . . . Sandy? . . . That's right. After a while, the plant would wilt and then die, because it needs water to *drink*, too.

We can see these leaves and how pretty they look, but there is another part of the plant that we can't see right now, but that's even more important. Do you know what that part is? . . .

Yes, it is the roots. They're down in the dirt, aren't they? And we must pour water into the dirt so the plant can drink. Then it will be healthy and will grow.

This reminds me of people. Some people are always thinking about how they look on the outside. They want to have pretty hair or a nice suntan, or they want to have nice clothes to wear.

This is all good, and it's all important. But it's not what is most important. We have something inside us that's just like the plant's roots. We have a heart, a mind, a soul. We can't see what's inside us any more than we can see the plant's roots that are inside the dirt. But they are there, and they are most important, and need to be cared for first.

I hope you're learning to think about what is inside people. People are special and beautiful, not because of what they look like on the outside, but because of what we know is inside.

Remember, the outside things that we see on people are important, and it's good to want to look nice on the outside. But that isn't as important as how people are on the inside, just as the plant's roots are more important than its leaves.

And remember that just as the water going into the ground will help the plant to have healthy roots, things like being loving and kind and honest will help us to "water" the important parts that are inside us.

---

27 · Guess Again

SCRIPTURE: *1 Corinthians 3:6—". . . but God gave the growth."*

OBJECT: *A glass jar, filled with a healthy snack treat*

CONCEPT: *We learn slowly, over time, about God's will for us, and we learn because God wants us to.*

Not long ago I saw a contest at a fair. There was a jar of pennies, and whoever guessed exactly how many pennies there were would win them. That looked like fun to me, but it looked hard, too, because there were no clues, and each person could only have one guess.

Today I thought we should do something like that here. I have brought with me a jar of green grapes. Do you like these? . . . I do too. They're one of my favorites, because they taste so good and I know they're good for me. Also, I know there aren't any seeds in them to worry about.

I want you to guess how many grapes there are in this jar. The right number is on the bottom, and if you guess, you may all have them to share.

There are two important things in this game, though, that are different from the game I saw at the fair. First of all, you may have as many guesses as you like. And secondly, I will give you clues as to whether your guess is too high or too low.

Okay, somebody take a guess. . . . Karen says twenty-five. That's too low. . . . Kevin says a hundred! That's too high. . . . That's closer . . . closer still. . . . Ah, good, Matt, you got it! Fifty-six! . . . What, Adam? Is that the number you were going to guess, too? Yes, there are fifty-six grapes in this jar, and each of you may have three of them. While you're getting your grapes, I want you to think about what this can teach us.

First of all, I want us to think about how long it took us to guess. It took many guesses, didn't it? We look at our Bibles, and they look very big sometimes, don't they? Nobody can learn about the Bible, or about God, or about how God wants us to live, in just a day or two. It takes many days and weeks and years, as we slowly learn more and more. That's why it's important to continue to come to church, and to continue to try to learn always.

The other thing I want us to remember is the clues I gave you, because I wanted you to find the answer and to have the grapes. God wants us to learn what is best, and to enjoy the good things in life. And so God leads us to learn more and more, and to grow a bit more each day as children of God.

Whenever you eat grapes like these from now on, I hope they'll remind you of the game we played today. Remember that God wants us to learn what is good in life. Remember also that it takes time to learn more and more about God, and that's why we try to keep on learning, week after week.

PENTECOST

A Season of Growing

28 · *The Language of Love*

SCRIPTURE: *Ephesians 4:15—"Speaking the truth in love, we are to grow up in every way into him who is the head, into Christ."*
OBJECT: *(A baby, six to nine months of age)*
CONCEPT: *We grow in a knowledge of God's love by being with persons who show us that love.*

This morning I'm going to ask Jenny to bring our son up here to be with us. Here he is! It looks as though he's happy to be with us, the way he's smiling, doesn't it?

Nevin is a little over six months old now, and he's beginning to make many different sounds. He's already trying to use his voice, and it won't be long before he'll start talking, will it?

I want to tell you, though, that I've been worrying about this. The other day I was reading a book that told about all the different languages that are spoken in the world, and I found out that there are hundreds of different ones that people speak. Do you know what some of the different languages are? . . . Very good, Chris; Spanish is a language. . . . Yes, Jeff, there is Chinese. . . . Good, Russian is also a language. And there are many languages spoken in Africa, and many different ones spoken by native Americans.

There are so many different languages, but I just speak English. I'm worried because with all those different languages in our world, Nevin might speak one of those instead of English, and I won't be able to talk with him!

Why are some of you shaking your heads? . . . Because Nevin will learn English, and I don't need to worry? Why? . . . I think you're right. Nevin will learn English because that's what he'll hear all around him.

We learn to speak a certain language because we hear it all around us. And we learn to be loving and kind when there is love all around us. I want us to remember how important it is to be with people who are loving, and who help us learn about God's love. It's important to be in places like our church, for example, where we are with loving people, and where we learn to be kind to one another.

I'm glad to know that Nevin will learn to speak the same language I do. I hope you'll also remember something from today—that it's important to be with people who show God's love, so we can learn about that love.

And I hope all of you will remember how important it is for you to set good examples for Nevin, and for all the other children who are younger than you, so they can grow up to know God's love too.

This text can be changed somewhat, or added to, at the time of an infant's baptism, to help the children understand how the baby will grow up in the promises the parents are making for him or her that day.

29 · *The Domino Theory of Patience*

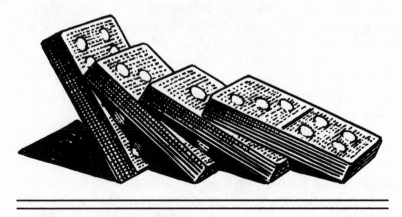

SCRIPTURE: *Romans 8:25—".* . . *we wait for it with patience."*

OBJECTS: *A box of dominoes and a small table*

CONCEPT: *When we learn to be patient and to wait, we sometimes find greater joy than we otherwise would have found.*

Do any of you like to play dominoes? . . . Do you? So do I. But do you know what? Sometimes I think it's even more fun to play *with* the dominoes than to play the dominoes game.

I have a little table here, and I'm going to set the dominoes up in a row. . . . Do you like to do that too, Jeff? . . . Good. . . . And some of the rest of you, too. Yes, this can be fun to do.

But do you know what? This is so much fun that sometimes I just can't wait to knock them down! . . . See, I did it again! I knocked down all four that I had set up in a row. That was fun to watch, wasn't it?

What, Steven? . . . I see. If I could wait until I had a long line of them, then it would be even more fun, wouldn't it?

This reminds me of something the Bible tells us. The Bible talks about "patience." That means being able to wait a little bit longer for something. Sometimes we aren't very happy to wait, or we don't understand why we should have to wait. But if we do, maybe something even better will happen, because God may have something very special planned for us, and we can find out what it is only by being willing to wait and see. That's patience.

. . . What, Lindsay? . . . Very good! That's right. People in the hospital are called "patients" too, aren't they? That's because people in the hospital need to wait each day while they get better. That is why they're called "patients."

Look, I have a long line of dominoes now. We were very patient, and now we have something very special. Who'd like to start them so they'll fall down? Okay, Becca.

I hope you'll remember our dominoes, and how much more fun they were when we waited until we had a long line. When we have patience, and wait a little bit longer, it's even more fun to play. So many times we find that God has even better things planned for us, if we just have patience to wait and find out what they may be.

30 · *Getting Better*

SCRIPTURE: *1 Peter 5:7—"[God] cares about you."*
OBJECT: *(A little cut or scratch that is now nearly healed)*
CONCEPT: *The miracle of our healing from little physical wounds is one of many ways that God shows love for us.*

Do any of you have a pet? . . .

We have a pet too. We have a cat, and the other day I was playing with her. Do you know what happens sometimes when you are playing with a cat, and you get too rough with it? . . . That's right! Sometimes, if we aren't careful, a cat might scratch us with its claws!

Well, that's what happened to me the other day. I was playing with my cat—whose name is Burger—and she scratched me right on the arm! And today I'm going to pull up my sleeve, so you can all see what a terrible condition I'm in! . . . Why, I wonder what happened to it? I'm sure there was a scratch on this arm. You do believe me, don't you? I'm sure it was right here.

Oh, here it is! But what's happened here? This scratch is so small now that I can hardly see it, and it just doesn't

look so bad now. Look at my scratch. I don't understand
this at all. The other day it looked so big and bad, but now
it doesn't. What do you think happened? . . .

David says that it's healed. How could that be? . . . I
see. . . . It just gets better. What makes it get better? . . .
Laurie says *God* helps it get better. Do you think she's
right? . . . Yes, I do too.

God has made each one of us so we have bodies that
can heal themselves from cuts and scratches and bruises.
And God has done this because God wants us to be healthy
and happy. When we have a cut or scratch, it doesn't just
stay forever, because God loves us and helps us be healed.

From now on, whenever we have a cut or a bruise or a
scratch, and we see that it's getting better, let's remember
that that's just one more way we can see how much God
loves us.

31 · Follow-ups: II

SCRIPTURE: *Luke 2:52—"And Jesus increased in wisdom and in stature, and in favor with God and [people]."*

OBJECTS: *A measuring stick, about five feet tall, and a marker (the stick does not need to have feet or inches marked on it, but you must be able to write on it; also, if you have a large number of children, you may want to have a second stick, and a helper to assist you in measuring some of the children)*

CONCEPT: *Even though we cannot always see it, we are growing every day—and it is God's loving care that makes us grow.*

Have each child stand by the measuring stick, and mark his or her height and name on it. Talk with the children about how they have all grown to be the height they are, and ask them what things help them grow. They should name food, fresh air, exercise, and rest. Help them see that all these are parts of God's plan, and that it is God's love, working through these things, that makes us grow. Talk to them about how Jesus grew, just as they are growing; relate the scripture to them. This can lead to discussion about other ways they are also growing—in knowledge, in learning various skills, and so forth.

The follow-up comes several months later, when you get the measuring stick out and mark their new heights on it. Compare them to see how they have grown, and talk to the children again about the miracle of growth, which is part of God's love.

It is a good idea to display the measuring stick or sticks in the lobby or narthex of the church after worship. This will allow the adults to see how the children have been growing, to share more of the excitement of that miracle, and to affirm the children further by talking with them individually about it.

32 · Free to Go

SCRIPTURE: *Galatians 5:1—"For freedom Christ has set us free; stand fast therefore, and do not submit again to a yoke of slavery."*
OBJECT: *A glass jar with grass at the bottom and large holes in its lid*
CONCEPT: *Because God loves us, God grants us freedom. We keep our freedom by appreciating it and using it wisely.*

One of my favorite things to do on these warm summer evenings is to catch lightning bugs. Do any of you like to do that? . . . Oh, good. I thought so. After you catch lightning bugs, do you ever do what I do? Do you ever put them in a glass jar and watch them light up? . . . Good! I like that too! As a matter of fact, I've brought along a jar filled with some beautiful lightning bugs that I caught last night. You can see that my jar has grass and water on the bottom for them, and it has holes in the lid so they can get fresh air. Just look. . . .

Wait! I don't see any lightning bugs in here, do you? I wonder what could have happened to them? . . . Oh, Jason says I made the holes too big and they flew out of my jar. Do you think that's right? . . . Well, that must be it, but I still don't understand *why* they would want to leave. After all, my jar is pretty and clean, and I have grass for them and a few drops of water for them to drink. Why would they want to leave my jar? . . .

That's right, Sandy, the next time I should make the holes smaller, shouldn't I? But what about this time? Why did the lightning bugs want to get out? . . . Ah, yes, Stacey, it's because they want to be free.

All God's creatures want to be free—from little lightning bugs all the way to us big people.

We're celebrating a holiday this weekend. Do you know what it is? . . . That's right. All of you know. It is the Fourth of July—Independence Day. We're celebrating because we live in a country that is free, and this is our country's birthday.

One of the important freedoms that we have is our freedom to worship. All of us here this morning are using our special freedom to join together openly to worship God. We are glad for this freedom, because we know that all our freedom comes from God. God loves us and wants us to use our freedom to choose what is good.

We must never forget how important our freedom is. By being glad for our freedom, and by using it to choose what is best, we will always keep our freedom.

I hope that the lightning bugs will remind you in these days ahead of how God made all of us with a desire to be free. (If you catch lightning bugs, be sure to let them go free after an hour or so.) And I hope that you will remember that God loves us and wants us to be free. Let's remember by being thankful for our freedom, and by using it to choose the best things for our lives.

33 · "Water" We Thirsty For?

5/6/90 A.O.

SCRIPTURE: *James 2:15-16—"... and one of you says to them, 'Go in peace ...'"*

OBJECT: *A plant, obviously in need of water*

CONCEPT: *Kind words are good, but we must go beyond kind words, to act out of our kindness, to show God's love.*

How many of you have heard of talking to plants? ... Quite a few of you have. This is the idea that plants grow better and are prettier when we talk to them—when we say nice things to them and let them know that we like them.

Do any of you believe that this is true—that it helps to talk to our plants? ... Good, I'm glad, because I believe it too.

I have a plant here that I want to show you. I must say, though, that I don't understand what is happening. I have been talking and talking to it, but it just isn't looking very healthy. For a while, it looked fine, but now it is looking worse and worse each day. Come on, plant. I like you so much and think you are beautiful. Get green and healthy again! . . .

What? What do you mean, I'm forgetting something? What am I forgetting? Oh, Kyle says I need to give some water to the plant. Do the rest of you think I need to water the plant? . . . You do? . . . But I've been talking and talking to it. I thought I wouldn't have to worry about watering it if I talked to it enough.

I have a glass of water here. T.J., would you like to give it a drink with me? . . . Thanks. I think the plant is going to be much better with this water, and think all of you were right about what it needed.

People are like this too. It's nice to say kind words to someone, but sometimes kind words alone aren't enough. Sometimes we have to *do* something to help, just as we had to give some water to our plant, and not just talk to it.

Maybe you know people who are lonely and would love to have a friend. It's nice to say to them that we hope they'll find a friend. But the best thing of all is to *be* a friend for them.

It's nice to talk about hoping that hungry children around the world will get something to eat. But it's much better to do something to help them. That's why I'm glad that some of you are helping to collect for UNICEF this week, because you are really doing something to help the hungry children.

The next time you help water the plants at your house, or see someone else watering the plants, I hope it will remind you of our talk today. Remember that it's nice to say kind words—but it's even better when we can *do* something kind.

34 · Rings Around the Roses

AW luve HN

SCRIPTURE: *Matthew 25:15—"To one he gave five talents, to another two, to another one."*

OBJECTS: *Pull rings from the tops of cans*

CONCEPT: *God has put potential that can be used for good or for bad into each of the things God has given us.*

I'll bet all of you know what these are. . . . That's right. They are the pull rings from the tops of cans. Do you think these are good things? Do you think that the person who invented these had a good idea? . . .

Yes, I think so too. These are good things, because they make it easy to open a can and get something to drink. We can go on a picnic and not worry about taking anything special along to open our cans of root beer if they have these rings on the top! So these are good things.

But do you know what? Do you know where I found all these rings? I found them all in the park, in the middle of a pretty flower bed. That is really sad. Some people threw all these on the ground—and then they turned into litter.

Many of these are thrown down on the ground, and they just stay there—and that's very bad. I've seen them at the beach, and people can sometimes step on them, and maybe cut their feet on them.

So these rings are very good things—and yet they can be very bad things, too. It all depends on how we use them.

God gives us many different things in our world. And do you know what? Just about everything that God gives us can be used for good, or for bad.

God gives many things to each one of us. We each have a brain—and we can use that brain to think of good things or of bad things. We each have energy—and we can use it to do good things or bad things. We can write or draw or talk or do all sorts of things. And every time, it is the same. We can use our gift from God in a good way or in a bad way.

Remember that God loves us, and God wants us to choose to do good things with all the special gifts that we have.

The next time you see someone opening a can with one of these, remember what a good thing it is. And the next time you see one lying on the ground, remember how things that can be good are often used in bad ways.

Maybe we could make it a point to pick these up whenever we see them lying on the ground, and throw them into a trash can. Or, better still, maybe we could take them to a recycling center. Every time we pick one of these up, it can remind us that God loves us and has given us so many good things—and that we want to do good things with everything God gives us.

35 · *It's What's in Mind That Counts!*

SCRIPTURE: *Matthew 15:11—"[It is] not what goes into the mouth [that] defiles . . . but what comes out."*

OBJECT: *The story below, acted out however possible*

CONCEPT: *Our intentions matter to God even more than our actions.*

I want to tell you about what happened to my friend Joyce this past week, and I hope that you'll be able to help me understand something about it. This is what Joyce told me happened.

Joyce's pencil needed to be sharpened, and her teacher told her that she could sharpen it. She started to walk back to her seat after she had sharpened it, and to get to her seat she had to walk past Wendy and Scott. Wendy thought it would be a good trick to make Joyce trip and fall down, so she stuck her foot out to trip her! But, luckily, Joyce saw what Wendy was trying to do, and she jumped out of the way in time!

Then, as Joyce kept on walking, Scott had to lean over

to pick up a paper he had dropped. His foot accidentally moved out and Joyce didn't see it—and she tripped and fell down!

And do you know what? Joyce was mad at Wendy, but she wasn't mad at all at Scott! Now I just don't understand this at all. After all, Scott was the one who actually tripped Joyce—not Wendy. So why would Joyce only be mad at Wendy? Can you help me understand this better? . . . Yes, thank you, April. I think that's exactly right. Joyce was mad at Wendy because she *wanted* to trip her, but she knew that Scott hadn't *meant* to, that it was only an accident.

One of the most important things that Jesus teaches us is that what we try to do is even more important than what we really end up doing. What we are *thinking* about doing and *wanting* to do is what counts most.

All of us do things that we don't want to do—sometimes. We may break something or forget something important. But if we did not *mean* to do it, then that's what matters. Maybe you have an older brother or sister who can make or buy your mother or father a much nicer birthday present than you can. But you know that you love your mom or dad just as much—and so does she or he know it—and that's what matters, even if you give a smaller gift.

Sometimes people may say something or do something that we don't like. But we must remember to think about whether they really wanted to say or to do that. Maybe they didn't mean it to be that way at all.

One of the important things about God's love is that it helps us to say and do what we really mean, and to understand that it's what we *want* to happen that matters most.

I hope you'll remember the story about Joyce, and I hope it will remind you that it is what we have in mind and want to do that counts most of all to God.

36 · Nuts on Knots!

SCRIPTURE: *Proverbs 15:1—"A soft answer turns away wrath, but a harsh word stirs up anger."*
OBJECT: *A shoe with a large knot in its laces*
CONCEPT: *A gentle approach is much stronger than a harsh or demanding one.*

Do you see what I have here? . . . Yes, it's a shoe, and it's one of my favorites. But do you see what's wrong with it? . . . Yes, it has a big knot in the shoestrings. Knots in shoestrings make me so mad! Look! The harder and harder I pull on these strings, the stronger and stronger the knot becomes! And it makes me feel even madder, so I pull even harder. But then the knot gets all the worse.

And do you know what? I finally get so mad that I just want to throw that old shoe away. "Who cares about it anyway?" I say.

Even when I'm mad and say that, though, I really do care about the shoe, and I don't want to throw it away. But what can I do? Do you think that all of us together could pull hard enough to make that knot come out? What do you think? . . . Oh, Deana says I should untie the knot. But how do I do that? It sounds very hard to me. . . . Oh, I see. I must pay attention and pull the string back through the knot to undo it. To do that we must take our time and be careful with it. . . . Look! Clinton is helping me get it out! Thank you, Clinton!

Do you know what this reminds me of? This reminds me how sometimes we have different ideas from our friends or maybe even a different idea from someone in our family about something. Sometimes that makes us mad, and it makes us want to argue with them or yell at them. But then the more we yell, the more they get mad, and the more they don't want to listen to us.

It's just like my knot. Pulling harder on it wouldn't untie it, and yelling louder at someone won't make him or her listen. Being gentle and careful and trying to understand the problem is what finally untied my knot. And being gentle and careful with other persons and trying to understand what they are thinking is what can get them to listen to us. That way we can still be friends. I don't think we want to lose our friends any more than I really wanted to throw away my shoe—even though I said so when I was mad.

God loves us, and God doesn't want us always to be yelling at each other. So God has made us in such a way that being gentle and kind with each other is the best way to get along.

The next time you have a knot in your shoe and you have to be careful about untying it, I hope it will remind you that we also must be gentle with each other to undo our problems.

37 · *Heavenly Hobbies*

SCRIPTURE: *1 Thessalonians 5:16-18—". . . Pray constantly. . . ."*

OBJECTS: *A book of matches and a silver dollar*

CONCEPT: *God loves all of us equally, but we see more of God's love when we pray often about our needs.*

Do any of you have hobbies? . . . Good! What about collections—do any of you collect certain things for a hobby? Danialle? You collect stamps? Very good. Roger, what about you? . . . Beer cans! I might have known that someone would!

I want to tell you a story this morning about two brothers who started collections. One boy's name was Keith, and he decided that he would collect different matchbooks, such as this one. His brother, named Paul, decided that he was going to collect silver dollars. After they started their collections, both of the boys asked their father if he would help them with their collections, and their father promised he would.

Well, as the days went by it seemed that nearly every day their father would bring home a new matchbook for

Keith. Sometimes he would even bring home two or three, depending on where he had been that day. And every once in a while—maybe once every two or three weeks—he would bring home a silver dollar for Paul's collection. Finally, Paul began to wonder why this was. Did his father love Keith more, since he brought home so many more things for Keith's collection?

What do you think? Why did their father give so much more to Keith than he did to Paul? . . . That's right, Sarah, it was because silver dollars are worth so much more, and it was much easier—and much fairer—to give more matchbooks.

I'm sure that Keith and Paul's father enjoyed giving them these things, and that he was glad Keith had chosen something that he could give often. He was glad to give the silver dollars to Paul, too, but probably wished he had chosen something that he could give more often.

This reminds me of how God loves us and wants to give things to us, just as the father in our story wanted to. God wants us to ask for what we need in our prayers.

Some people are a little bit like Paul, because they only pray for big things. Sometimes God answers one of those big prayers, but perhaps it doesn't seem to happen very often.

Other people have learned to pray every day, not only for big things, but for everything—for food for today, for help doing the right thing, for energy to play, and so forth. These people can see that God is always answering their prayers, and they can see each day how many good things they are receiving from God.

Remember that God wants to give to us, and remember that when we pray every day—for big things *and* for the little things we need—then we're able to see so much more of the good things that God wants to give us.

38 · Receiving from Giving

Kari ?

SCRIPTURE: *Luke 6:38—"Give, and it will be given to you; good measure, pressed down, shaken together, running over, will be put into your lap. For the measure you give will be the measure you get back."*
OBJECTS: *Bananas, in various conditions*
CONCEPT: *Giving not only brings good things to the person who is receiving, but also to the person who is giving.*

One of my favorite fruits is a banana. Do you like bananas too? . . . Yes, I like them especially on my cereal at breakfast. I like bananas when they are fresh and good, and do you know what helps keep them fresh? . . . That's exactly right, Tammy. The peel on each banana helps keep it fresh.

So the peel on a banana is very important. It keeps the banana from being bruised, and it keeps air and dirt and bugs out. We might say that a banana peel gives and gives to the banana to take care of it.

But I noticed something the other day that was very surprising. And I think it is very important, too. Here, let me show you what I discovered. Do you see this banana peel? It's from a banana I ate yesterday, and it came from the same bunch of bananas as this one here. But do you see how dark and wrinkled this peel is, compared to the peel that is still on the banana? Or look at this banana that was peeled and eaten halfway down. The peel where the banana is missing has begun to shrivel up, but the part of the peel that is still taking care of the banana is still nice and yellow.

Do you know what this reminds me of? This reminds me that giving is not only good for the person who is receiving, but also for the person who is doing the giving.

If I give something to you, Taryn, then that is good for you. But it's also good for me. It helps me to know how important it is to share. It helps me feel thankful for how much I have that I am able to share. And it gives me a very good feeling and helps me be happier. I don't know exactly how or why, but all this gives me energy and a good feeling about life.

As I said, I don't know exactly why all this is, but then I don't know exactly why the peel stays fresher when it is on the banana, either. I only know that God loves us and has made the world to be an especially nice place when we care about others and share with others.

When we give, we also receive.

The next time you eat a banana and notice how the peel has been taking care of the banana, remember that. Remember that it has been good for the peel, too.

39 · *If You Read the News You Know*

SCRIPTURE: *Romans 8:28—"In everything God works for good."*

OBJECT: *A newspaper*

CONCEPT: *We can understand some things, but not everything. How much we do understand helps us to realize even more how much more God understands, and to trust in God's will for us.*

Do any of you have a mom or a dad who sometimes says, "Oh, I just can't start my day until I read the newspaper"? . . . A couple of you do. Well, I thought you might, because some people just can't go through a day without reading the newspaper, and knowing what is going on. Do any of you like to read the paper? . . . Oh, you like to read the comics! That's good. Duff, you like to read the sports? I must say I read that page once in a while myself!

I've noticed something pretty amazing about newspapers. At first I thought it must just be an accident, but I've been checking every day and every day, and it's always true. Do you know what I've noticed that is always so amazing? It's that every day there is just enough news to fill each page of the paper!

Don't you think that's something? I would think that some days there wouldn't be quite enough news, so that there would be some empty space left. And I would think that on some other days there would be too much news, so that the words would have to be jammed around the edges. But no—every day there is just enough news for the number of pages.

Look—even when a story starts on the front page and it's very long, there's always just enough room to finish it on another page.

Now, what I want to figure out is *why*. Why is there always just enough news? What do you think? . . . I think Luella is right. The people who work at the paper fix it that way. What is the person called who fits all the stories onto the page, and makes sure that they're just the right length? . . . That's right, Danialle, that person is the editor.

There's a very important verse in our Bibles that talks about what God does. It says that God is a little bit like an editor in our lives. God loves us and wants everything to work together, to fit together in the best possible ways.

If people are able to put things like a newspaper together and make it fit just right, then think about how much more God can do. Even though we sometimes can't understand why something has happened, we still believe in God and still trust in God. We believe God will help everything to work together for something good to come about.

I hope that sometimes when you look at how stories fit together in a newspaper, it will remind you of how God helps things fit together and work out for the best in our lives.

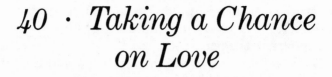

40 · Taking a Chance on Love

SCRIPTURE: *John 6:9—"There is a lad here who has five barley loaves and two fish. . . ."*
OBJECTS: *A packet of crayons and a pad of paper*
CONCEPT: *When we share, we are taking a risk, but we know that God blesses us in our sharing.*

Today we'll need two volunteers to talk about something very important. Let's see . . . Karyn and Becky, would you step up here? I want us to pretend today that Karyn and Becky both have something. Karyn has a pack of crayons and Becky has this tablet.

Now, while they're holding these for a minute, tell me, are crayons a good thing to have? . . . Yes, they are, Deana. We can draw things and color pictures with them. But are crayons any good without a coloring book or a pad or something like that? . . . No, they are not. We certainly don't want to color on the wall, or do anything like that, so they aren't very good alone.

What about paper from a pad? Can we use it alone? . . .

Yes, there are a few things we could fold and make with the paper. But it would be much nicer if we had some crayons to use with it, wouldn't it?

Look at Becky and Karyn. One has a tablet, but no crayons, and the other has crayons, but no tablet. What do you think should happen that would make it better for each one of them? Heather? . . . That's right. They should share with each other, and then they would have much more fun.

Sharing is good. That's very important to remember. But do you know what? There's something else to remember. And that is that someone has to be first. If Becky keeps waiting for Karyn to share, and Karyn keeps waiting for Becky to share, then nothing will ever happen. One of them has to be first. One of them has to go ahead, and take a chance that the other one will want to share too.

There is a story in our Bibles about a time that a big crowd of people came out to be with Jesus, and after a while all of them became hungry. There was one boy who had brought some fish and some bread for his lunch, and do you know what? He came up to Jesus and wanted to share his lunch with all those people!

That boy was taking a big chance, giving his lunch away like that. But then Jesus prayed to God and a miracle happened, and there was enough food for everyone.

God wants us to discover good things in our lives. When we are willing to be first to share whatever we have, a miracle may happen. We may find that we have even more because of our sharing.

Look. By sharing, Karyn and Becky now both have crayons and both have paper, and both of them can have more fun than before. Somebody always must be first to share, and sometimes that means we're taking a chance. But God blesses us when we share, just as the little boy who was willing to share his lunch with that crowd was blessed.

41 · Jewels from Junk

SCRIPTURE: *1 Corinthians 1:27—"But God chose what is foolish in the world. . . ."*
OBJECT: *A craft or art object made from scrap materials*
CONCEPT: *God is able to turn anything or anyone into something very special.*

I have something we've all seen many times—an old tin can. What good is a tin can after it's used? . . . That's right. It's not very much good at all. We'll probably just throw this can away, or maybe recycle it, so that new cans will be made from it. That's all I know to do with it.

There is someone in our church, though, who knows something else to do with old tin cans. Mrs. Freshley does something very special with them, and I want to show you what that is. First of all she has Mr. Freshley cut the can into strips so it looks like this. Then she rolls and twists the strips, bending each of them in a certain way.

Finally, after working and working, she makes . . . this! Look at this little chair! Isn't it beautiful? I'm going to hold it so that each of you can get a good look at it. Can you believe that this was made from an old tin can like this one? . . . It is hard to believe, isn't it? But it's true.

Sometimes we make a mistake, or we do something we wish we hadn't done—and then we begin to feel bad about ourselves. In times like that we may even begin to feel that we aren't much good. We may even feel like this old tin can over here.

But then—God is able to take us and help us to change into something beautiful and special, just as Mrs. Freshley helped change this can into a beautiful chair. As a matter of fact, when we're the saddest about ourselves can sometimes be the time that God will help us the most.

When you see a tin can, please remember what Mrs. Freshley does with old tin cans. And just think—if a person can do something this good with a can, what must God, who is so much greater, be able to do with each one of us?

Even when you're feeling sad about yourself for some reason, don't give up on yourself. Trust in God, because God loves you and will help you to become all the special things that you were created to be.

42 · *Tripped Up*

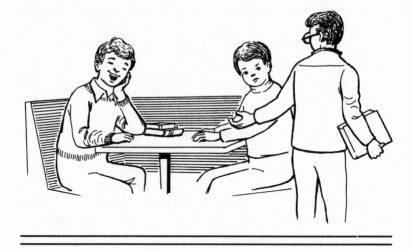

SCRIPTURE: *Galatians 5:7—"You were running well; who hindered you from obeying the truth?"*

OBJECT: *A tiny stone*

CONCEPT: *Bad habits that seem small can actually become very big, preventing us from having good things we hope to have.*

Do you see this? I hope you can see it. This is a tiny stone, smaller than the tip of my littlest finger. I have a story to tell you about this stone.

When I was in school, I had a friend who was a good runner for our track team. One day he was very sad, and he told me that he had lost his race that day—and he lost it because of a stone that was this big. Can any of you guess how a little stone like this could make someone lose a race? . . . Krissie? . . . No, he didn't slip on it. That's a good guess, though, because that sometimes happens, doesn't it? . . . Luella? . . . No, it didn't fly up and hit him, but that's another good guess. . . . Jeff? . . . Yes, that's right. It got into his shoe!

Have any of you ever gotten a stone in your shoe? . . .

Yes, of course, we all have. Well, my friend told me that a little stone got into his shoe, and then his foot hurt from it, and he just couldn't run very fast because it bothered him so much.

This makes me think about the sorts of habits we have. There are good habits—good things that we do each day or each week because we're used to doing them. There are also bad habits—things we start to do over and over that are not good.

I remember one time when I was a boy I got into the habit of saying things to make fun of people. I thought it was pretty funny, but after a while I noticed that people didn't want to be my friends any more because of the unkind things that I was in the habit of saying.

Sometimes we think, "Oh, that's just a little thing I've been doing. It couldn't hurt." But remember the stone in my friend's shoe. It was very little, but it made a big difference—and so can little habits.

The next time you get a little stone in your shoe, and it hurts in a big way, I know you'll want to take it out right away. While you do, think about this story from today. Think about how little habits can make a big difference. And think about the kinds of habits you are getting into in your life.

I hope they will be good ones.

43 · Balloons and Bags

SCRIPTURE: *1 Corinthians 2:1-12—"Now we have received . . . the Spirit which is from God, that we might understand the gifts bestowed on us."*
OBJECTS: *Several inflated balloons in a bag*
CONCEPT: *The church, by teaching values found in our scriptures, helps us to understand and coordinate the many parts of our lives.*

I think I'm pretty strong! To prove to you that I'm very strong, I'm going to pick this up. Look! You can see that this bag is just filled to overflowing with balloons! Now, don't you agree that this is pretty amazing? . . . Hmmm . . . You don't seem to be very impressed. . . . Balloons aren't very heavy? Well, maybe we need a volunteer to see if you can do as well. Matthew, would you like to step up here and see if you can do it? Thank you.

But, Matthew, you are such a *busy* person, with so many things on your mind. I don't think you should need to waste time with this old *bag*. It just means one more thing you have to hold. Here, let me just pour the balloons out into your arms and—oh, my! What's the matter? Why are you letting some of them fall on the floor? Are they too heavy for you? . . .

No, of course they aren't. That's right. It isn't that they are too heavy, but that there are too many of them, and Matthew can't get hold of all of them at once. Sit down a minute, Matt, while we talk about this.

You can see that different words are printed on these balloons. They say, "School," "Homework," "Chores," "Music Lessons," "Sports Teams," "Time with Family," "Clubs," "Time with Friends," and so forth. These are some of the things that I'll bet many of you have going on in your lives. Do any of you do any of these things? . . . Yes, I'm sure all of you do.

I hear some people say, "Oh, I'm so busy I just don't have time for church and Sunday school." But do you know what? The church can be just as this bag is to these balloons. That's why I've printed the word *Church* on the other side of this bag. God has given us many special things to do in our lives, but God wants us to enjoy all these things and not get all confused and worn out. That's why the Bible teaches us so many lessons about what is most important, and how we should best use our time. At the church we study God's word in the Bible, and that helps us to learn what is most important—how to "get hold of our lives." So even though it takes more of our time to come to church and Sunday school, it can actually help us to have more time for ourselves by teaching us what is most important and most worth our time.

Look, the balloons are in the bag now, and Matthew can lift them easily. The balloons weren't too heavy for him. He just needed a way to get hold of all of them. I'll bet any of you could lift this bag now. . . .

While some of you are doing that, I'm going to give a balloon to each of you to take home. When you play with it, I hope it will remind you of what we have talked about this morning.

44 · *Learning Is Worth It!*

June 91-AO.

SCRIPTURE: *John 11:10—"If any one walks in the night, he stumbles, because the light is not in him."*

OBJECTS: *Three clean sheets of paper, two ordinary pencils, and a pencil with an eraser on both ends (if you do not have such an object, simply make one with a little tape)*

CONCEPT: *Sometimes it is difficult, but it is worth the effort to learn and to use fully the talents God has given us.*

Lately I've been trying to learn to draw. Have any of you ever drawn anything? Good! Maybe you'll be able to help me learn too. I'm going to take this pencil and paper and try to learn to draw a house and a yard. *(Draw the house quickly, with windows up in the air, clouds underneath the house, an upside-down "stick man" outside, and so forth.)*

Well, what do you think of my drawing? . . . You don't think it's very good! Well, what's wrong? . . . Oh, I see. Well, I think I'll take a new pencil and a new piece of paper, and try again. I'll bet my problem was just that I had the wrong pencil! *(Draw another scene with more mistakes, and, a bit more quickly, repeat the process.)*

Well, I don't know if I'll ever learn to draw. Maybe I'll try one more pencil. Why, this pencil *(the one with the two erasers)* looks just right for me! *(Try to "draw" with one of its ends.)* Look, I can't make any mistakes drawing now. This pencil is perfect for my drawing, because I don't make any more mistakes, the way I did before. Don't you agree that this is good? *(Let them think about it for a moment.)*

What? Barbie doesn't think this is a good pencil for me to use. Why not? . . . That's right. It's because I'm not drawing anything with it. I'm not making any more mistakes, but I'm not learning this way, either.

Sometimes when we try to learn something new, it's hard at first, isn't it? And sometimes we just want to give up. But we never learn anything if we don't keep trying. God has made each one of us so that we are able to learn to do many different things. What are some of the things that you've learned to do that were hard for you to learn at first? . . . Those are some good things to be able to do, and I'm proud of you for trying and for learning them.

Let's be glad for all the things we can do—like drawing. And let's be glad for all the other new things we can learn. Let's keep trying, even when it's hard, because learning is worth it!

45 · Peaches and Prayers

SCRIPTURE: *Acts 10:31—"Cornelius, your prayer has been heard."*
OBJECTS: *Two peaches, one obviously riper than the other*
CONCEPT: *Even though there are millions of people praying, God still hears each individual.*

Good morning to all of you! And it is a good and beautiful morning, isn't it? One of the reasons it's such a good morning is that the sun is shining so brightly, and it makes everything so pretty.

Tell me—how important is the sun? . . . That's right, the sun is very important. Scientists tell us that without the sun, we couldn't stay alive for more than a few minutes. The sun gives us heat. Every day, the whole world is kept warm by the sun. Even when it's cloudy and we can't see the sun, even in the winter when we think it's cold—even then the sun is shining on the world and keeping it as warm as it is. The sun is very, very important.

This past week my wife, Jenny, had an idea I thought was pretty silly. We had some peaches that weren't ripe enough to eat, and she wanted us to be able to eat them for dessert that night. So she took them outside and set them in the sunshine so they would get riper.

I said to her, "Jenny, don't be silly. The sun is much too busy to be bothering with peaches. The sun has to keep the whole world warm so we can all live. It certainly doesn't have time to help us ripen a couple of peaches!"

Do you think I was pretty smart to tell her that? Don't you think I was right? . . . Well, Jenny wouldn't listen to me. She took the peaches out anyway and set them in the sun. . . . And do you know what? They became riper and riper from the sunlight! As busy as the sun is, doing things all over the world, it took time to ripen our peaches as if it had nothing else to do!

Sometimes people wonder how God can hear our prayers. God is so busy and so great. Especially when so many of us are praying all at the same time, we wonder how God can hear all our prayers at once.

God does hear our prayers, though, and I think the sun can help us to understand better how that can be. God is greater than the sun, even more important to us than the sun. God gives us life and everything that we have in our lives. Yet God takes time to hear each one of us when we pray, just as the sun takes time to ripen our peaches and grapes and tomatoes.

God hears us because God is love. Whenever you are eating something that is juicy and ripe from the sun, I hope it will remind you of our lesson today. I hope you will always remember that anytime we turn to God in prayer, our prayers are heard and understood.

46 · In the Bag!

SCRIPTURE: *Isaiah 55:9—"For as the heavens are higher than the earth, so are my ways higher than your ways and my thoughts higher than your thoughts."*
OBJECTS: *A plastic sandwich bag and a banana*
CONCEPT: *No matter how smart people are, there are many things that we cannot do as well as God.*

Do all of you know what this is? Of course, it's a plastic bag. What are plastic bags used for, Kristen? . . . That's right. They're used to keep food fresh. I'll bet some of you even put sandwiches and other things for your lunch in these, don't you?

I like plastic bags. They're neat and clean, so nice and clear. I think whoever invented these is pretty smart, and I like to use them whenever I can.

All of you know what this is, too, don't you? . . . Of course, it's a banana. What is the peel of a banana good for? . . . That's exactly right. It keeps the banana inside it fresh. Do you know what, though? Sometimes banana peels aren't very pretty. Sometimes they get black spots on them, or other stains or marks on them, and I don't like them so much then.

But, I have a very good idea, and I need your help for it. I think this afternoon all of us should go to the supermarket and all the other grocery stores, and we'll peel all the bananas and throw those old peels away. Then we'll put all those bananas into plastic bags instead. I think they'll look so much nicer then, don't you? How many of you want to go with me and help me put all the bananas into plastic bags?

What? Only one or two of you? Wait a minute. Why don't you want to help me? . . . You say the plastic bags wouldn't keep them as fresh? What else? Roger? . . . Ah, that's right. The bananas are big and little and slightly different in shape, and the plastic bags are all exactly the same. So the bags wouldn't fit each banana just right, but the banana peels are always the exact size and shape to keep the banana fresh.

I really don't think I will put the bananas into plastic bags, because you're right. That would be a silly thing to do. Even though plastic bags are a wonderful invention, they just can't be as good as what God has made. No matter how smart we are, and no matter what we invent, we still aren't as smart as God, or able to do many of the things that God does.

I hope the next time you peel a banana and notice how fresh it is inside, you'll be reminded of the many wonderful things that God has given us.

47 · A Dull Diet

SCRIPTURE: *Genesis 1:29—"Behold, I have given you every plant yielding seed which is upon the face of all the earth . . . ; you shall have them for food."*
OBJECT: *A box of raisins*
CONCEPT: *God has given us many good things, and we learn and grow best by experiencing as many of them as we can.*

All of you know what's in this box, don't you? . . . That's right—raisins! Who knows what raisins are made from? Corey? . . . That's right; raisins are grapes that are dried in the sun. Do any of you like raisins? . . . All of you do! Good, while we talk I'll let each of you take a handful of them. . . .

Tell me, are raisins good for us? . . . Yes, they are. Grapes are very nutritious, and all that sunshine puts vitamin D into them. So it is very good for us to eat raisins— much better than eating candy for a snack.

Right now, our little boy, Nevin, likes raisins for his favorite food. He asks for them at every meal, and whenever he wants a snack he always thinks of raisins. As a matter of fact, I think that if we would let him, he would eat nothing but raisins. Do you think that would be a good idea? Do you think it would be good if Nevin ate nothing else but raisins? . . .

No? Why not? We've said that raisins are very good for us, haven't we? . . . Tammy? . . . That's right. It wouldn't be good for us to eat just one thing. We need different kinds of healthy foods in order to have healthy bodies. That's why God has given us many different things to eat.

We need different kinds of things to be healthy in our bodies *and* in our minds. That's a good thing to remember. For example, I think that Sunday school is a very good place to be. But I wouldn't want all of you to be here for Sunday school every minute of every day! You need to be at home and at school and out playing and at Sunday school. You need different kinds of good things to grow in the best ways.

You need different friends too. You may have one very special friend that you enjoy playing with the most, but it would not be good to be with him or her every minute. You learn different things by being with different friends.

Remember that even though raisins are good for us, they can't make us healthy by themselves. Remember that we also need different kinds of good friends and good places to come to, in order to be as healthy as we can be in our minds and our hearts.

We are very thankful that God loves us and has put so many different, good things in our world for us to have and to use, so that we can grow in healthy and happy ways.

48 · God's Wonderful World

SCRIPTURE: *Psalm 111:2—"Great are the works of [God]"*
(or Psalm 8:3-4, or any other psalm or other scripture
that proclaims wonder at God's world).

OBJECTS: *Charts, pictures, or other objects that show the*
lesson you wish to share

CONCEPT: *God has created a wonderful and amazing world*
for us to discover.

It was a great day for me when I realized that many children's sermons—especially in the warm months of the Pentecost season—could simply be times of discovering and discussing some of the many facets of our world of nature.

Some things that can be the topic of conversation with the children are the water cycle (how and why God causes water to evaporate, form clouds and rain, etc.); the life of any part of the animal kingdom (particularly those that provide us with very colorful pictures); leaves (how and why they fall); or even the solar system or stars (but be very careful to keep this on a basic level that they will be able to comprehend).

Whatever creative method the worship leader can develop to introduce and lead these sessions is fine. Always be sure to have as the emphasis a sense of wonder at the beautiful and amazing world God has given us.

These can be good sermons for several reasons: they give the children opportunity to share some things they have been learning in school; they can give new insights into the beauty and complexity of God's plan for the world (the water cycle cleanses the water and air, as well as giving us different kinds of weather); and, because they deal with topics that are often day-to-day encounters for the children, the lessons of these sermons should often come to mind for them.

49 · In Small Packages

SCRIPTURE: *Luke 17:6—"If you had faith as a grain of mustard seed . . ."*
OBJECT: *A battery from an electronic watch*
CONCEPT: *It is not outward size but inner qualities that give us our value.*

The other day I heard something that made me very sad. I heard some boys making fun of another boy, just because he wasn't as big as they were. They were teasing him about the things he couldn't do, and things he couldn't reach, and so forth. I was especially sad about this, because I know that boy, and I know what a nice person he is. He does many helpful things for his mom and dad and other people. So I think he is really pretty big on the *inside*. Do you know what I mean by this? . . .

Let me show you something. Do you know what this is? . . . No, that's a good guess, Joshua, but it isn't quite right. This is a battery. That's right. I would never have guessed what it was, either, until someone told me. This is the kind of battery that is used in watches, like this one. This little battery, which is barely the size of my smallest fingertip, has so much energy packed into it that it can make this watch keep perfect time for a whole year! Think about that! This will keep a watch running all the way through the school year, and the summer too!

That's a very big thing to do, isn't it? I would say that even though this battery looks small, it's really very big, because of what's inside it, and because of what it can do from what's inside it.

One of the things Jesus wanted us to understand is that it is not what a person looks like, or how big he is, or what color her skin is that matters. What's on the outside doesn't matter so much, Jesus taught us. It's what is inside us that counts the most. If we're filled with God's love, and if we're filled with belief in God and confidence in ourselves from that faith in God, then we are very special, and then we can do some pretty big things.

I hope you'll remember that. It's not what is outside, but what is inside a person that matters most. Remember my little battery that does such big things. Remember that it is God's great love for us that we feel in our hearts and minds that makes us very special.

50 · *The Key of Keys*

SCRIPTURE: *2 Timothy 3:17—". . . that the [people] of God may be complete, equipped for every good work."*

OBJECTS: *Three sets of keys*

CONCEPT: *The Bible gives us insight and direction for all aspects of living.*

We have talked at times in the past about how Jesus liked to tell riddles, which we call parables. He liked to tell them because they made people think—and because they were fun, and Jesus liked to have fun.

I have a riddle for you today. The riddle is: What question can you never answer "yes" to? What question do you think that might be? . . . It is, "Are you asleep?" Some of you had good guesses. Would you like to ask me a riddle now? Heather? . . . Why can't you fool a snake? I don't know. Why not? . . . Because you can't pull its leg! That's very good! Riddles are fun, aren't they?

I have a story today that's like a riddle, and I want to see if you can answer it for me.

A woman had so many keys that she decided to keep them on three different key rings. On one ring she kept the

---

keys for her car. On another ring she kept her keys for work. And on the other ring she kept the keys to her house.

One day she was about to go to work. Her house was locked and her car was locked. Then she was just about to get into her car when she realized that in her handbag she had only *one* of her rings of keys, and that the others were inside her house. As she pulled out the ring that she had in her bag, she hoped that it would be one certain ring of keys.

Now, which ring of keys do you think she was hoping they were? . . . The car keys? That's a very good guess, because then she could drive her car, couldn't she? But I don't think that's the best answer.

Becky? . . . Yes, that's right; she hoped they would be her house keys. Why? . . . Yes, because then she could get *all* her keys, and drive her car and get into her work building too. So her house keys were the most important, because they would help her to have all the keys.

This riddle or parable makes me think of the Bible, because it's the most important book we have. It's a key for life. There are many important books that tell us about different things, but the Bible tells us many, many things. It teaches us about God and the stories of Jesus. It also teaches us about ourselves and how we should treat other people. It teaches us things that will help us understand what is right to do in all sorts of different situations.

I hope you'll remember that Jesus liked riddles, and that when you hear or tell a riddle it will remind you of our riddle today about the keys. Maybe you could tell it to your friends and see if they can answer it. And tell them what we've talked about today—that the Bible is like the key to the house, because it helps us to have all the keys.

4-3-94

51 · Chores for Baby

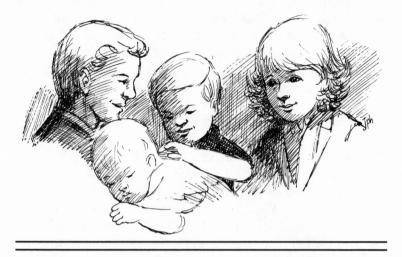

SCRIPTURE: *Romans 5:6—"While we were yet helpless . . ."*
OBJECT: *(An infant)*
CONCEPT: *God loves us not for what we do, but for who we are.*

Someone very special is being brought up to be with us this morning—our new son, Caleb. Caleb is five weeks old now, and we are very proud of him, and love him very much. Can all of you see him if I hold him right here? Good. Some of you have new babies in your families now too, don't you? Lynnie does, and so does Chad.

My wife, Jenny, and I love Caleb so much, and do you know why? It's because he does the dishes, and mows the lawn, and takes out the garbage every day, and . . .

What?! What do you mean you don't believe Caleb does all these things? Todd, doesn't Megan do all those things at your house? No? What about the rest of you? You believe Caleb helps us with all those chores, don't you?

. . . Well, I'm afraid I have to admit that you're right. Caleb doesn't help with the lawn-mowing or the garbage or the dishes. He doesn't help with any of the housework at all. As a matter of fact, we have to feed him, and get up in the night to take care of him, and change his diapers! We have to do all sorts of extra work because of him, and he doesn't do anything for us!

. . . But do you know what? We still love Caleb so, so much, even though he doesn't do anything to *earn* our love. Why do you think that is? . . . That's right, Kevin. We love him just because he's our son. That's all the reason there is.

Do you know what? God loves us that much, too, and even more. God loves us even before we're old enough to love God in return. God loves us even before we're old enough to do good things for God.

Remember that God loves you just as your parents love you—just as we love Caleb. They love you just because you are their children, and not because of what you do.

But then, when we know how much our parents love us, and how much God loves us, then we do good things in return—not because we have to, but because we want to. We hope that someday Caleb will want to do good things for us—and that will make us very happy. I know that it makes your parents very happy when you want to do good things to help them. Remember that.

But most of all, remember that God loves you—and your parents love you—for who you are. You are their children, and you are God's children. That means you are very special—and very much loved.

52 · The First Thanksgiving

SCRIPTURE: *Philippians 4:4-13—"I have learned, in whatever state I am, to be content."*

OBJECTS: *The following story and questions (hats or other Pilgrim dress or symbols can also be used to add to the story)*

CONCEPT: *The most important reasons for thanksgiving are the many blessings of God's love—which God has always shared with people.*

This story can be read to the children and discussed with them on the Sunday preceding Thanksgiving, or as part of a special Thanksgiving Eve or Thanksgiving Day service. The discussion questions that follow the story are most important in the time with the children.

I want you all to imagine with me that it is about the year 1620—over 350 years ago. We are going back to the time of the first Thanksgiving in America. We are going to be visiting a Pilgrim family named Bradford—with Mr.

Bradford, Mrs. Bradford, and their children, Abe and Sarah.

"Children! Abe and Sarah!" called Mrs. Bradford. "You'd better get up now!"

Abe and Sarah were still quite sleepy as they looked at their clocks. And were they surprised! Why, it was nearly nine o'clock! Abe and Sarah were not used to sleeping so late. All summer they had to get up to help with the chores, and now that school had started, they always had to be up by seven, because the school bus came very early.

"I would have let you sleep as long as you wanted," said Mrs. Bradford, "but the parades are going to begin on television at ten o'clock, and I know you don't want to miss them."

"Oh, boy!" said Sarah, "I want to see the Mayflower Parade! It's always the best, and it's in color, too!"

So the children put on their black-and-white clothes and their shoes with buckles. Sarah wore her bonnet, and Abe put on his black Pilgrim hat. Then the whole family watched the parades together, and they were very happy.

When the parades were over, Mr. Bradford said, "My, in honor of the first Thanksgiving today we really should do something special. But what shall we do?"

"I know!" shouted Abe. "There's a football game today between the Chiefs and the Redskins. Let's watch them play."

At first it seemed like a good idea, but then Mrs. Bradford thought it would be better if the family spent the afternoon at home, playing games together, having family worship, and giving thanks for the ways that God had taken care of them that first year in America. Everyone else thought that would be a good idea.

"But let's eat first," said Abe. "I'm hungry."

"Yes, that would be a good idea," said Mr. Bradford.

"But I don't know what to fix," said Mrs. Bradford. "We've never had a Thanksgiving before, and I don't know what to serve for the occasion."

So the family thought and thought, and finally Sarah said, "Whatever we have, I think we should invite the Indians and all our other friends and neighbors, too." That was certainly a good idea, but the family still didn't know what to eat.

Then Abe shouted, "I know! Let's go to the pizza parlor!"

And so they did. The Bradford family went, and so did all their Pilgrim friends and neighbors; and instead of playing football, the Chiefs went too. They had a happy time together, and they all were very thankful as they ate their special Thanksgiving pizzas. On their pizzas they had cheese, mushrooms, pepperoni, and lots of cranberries!

And that is the story of the first Thanksgiving.

Questions for the Children

Is this the way the first Thanksgiving really happened?

How do you know? What was the first Thanksgiving really like?

If the Pilgrims didn't have television, football, pizzas, and some of the other things we have now, how could they be thankful, and why would they want to have a Thanksgiving celebration?

What are some of the things the Pilgrims had that we also have, that are the most important things—and the most important reasons for being thankful?

INDEX OF SCRIPTURES